Greetings from Spitsbergen

Tourists at the Eternal Ice 1827–1914

John T. Reilly

Greetings from Spitsbergen

Tourists at the Eternal Ice 1827–1914

tapir academic press

© Tapir Academic Press, Trondheim 2009
ISBN   978-82-519-2460-3

This publication may not be reproduced, stored in a retrieval system or transmitted in any form or by any means; electronic, electrostatic, magnetic tape, mechanical, photocopying, recording or otherwise, without permission.

Layout: Bjørg Daugstad Wik, Tapir Academic Press
Paper: Artic Volume 115 g
Printing and binding: 07 Gruppen as

Cover painting: Andrée's base camp (private collection)
Cover photography: "Auguste Victoria's" tourists, Bellsund, 1897

Tapir Academic Press publishes textbooks and academic literature for universities and university colleges, as well as for vocational and professional education. We also publish high quality literature of a more general nature. Our main product lines are:

- Textbooks for higher education
- Research and reference literature
- Non-fiction

We only use environmentally certified printing houses.

Tapir Academic Press
NO–7005 Trondheim, Norway
Tel.:   + 47 73 59 32 10
Email: post@tapirforlag.no
www.tapirforlag.no

Publishing Editor: laila.andreassen@tapirforlag.no

Index

Acknowledgements 7

Tourist Post 9

The Pioneers 31

English Cruises 41

Wilhelm Bade's Cruises 67

Norwegian Cruises 103

German Cruises 129

French Cruises 161

Postcards as Snapshots in History 173

Appendix A: Tourist Stamps (Etiquettes) 189

Appendix B: Spitsbergen's Tourist Ships (1881–1914) 195

Appendix C: Explanation of Place-Names 215

Bibliography 223

Acknowledgements

I am deeply indebted to Chris Gibson, Phil Hubbard and Angus Erskine who, in their own individual ways, helped sow the seeds for this project. I am also very grateful to all those who kindly replied to my endless queries for information. I would like to give special thanks to Klaus Berthelmess, whose encyclopaedic knowledge of whaling helped clarify a number of issues; John Showell, who kindly provided biographical details, as well as a portrait of captain Max Dietrich from his late wife's estate; Freerk Rosenblaum, an "Oihonna" *aficionardo*, who helped open my eyes to new lines of enquiry and Frank Berger, curator of the Historical Museum of Frankfurt am Maine, for allowing me to reproduce photographs relating to Lerner and his rescue of the "Ile-de-France". I am also grateful to Heide and Maritas Bodensohn, granddaughters of Frank Lerner, for providing details of the "Thalia" and to Patricia Adams and Alan Totten, for giving of their time and sharing with me their enthusiasm and knowledge of postcards and cruise mail. I would also like to thank Beat Stutzer and Alexandra Käz of the Bündner Kunstmuseum for providing biographical details and copies of Hans Beat Wieland's works; the Wiltshire Historical Society for information relating to John Du Boulay, David Newman of the Goldhangar Historical Society for details relating to the Northern Exploration Society and Diane Marriott for help in tracking down obscure references.

Every effort has been undertaken to contact all copyright holders. For the use of copyright materials and permission to consult and refer to primary sources, my most grateful acknowledgements to the Bodleian Library, Oxford; British Library, London; Grenna Museum, Grenna; Kungl. Biblioteket, Stockholm; Nasjonalbiblioteket, Oslo; National Maritime Museum, London; Marquette County Historical Society, Michigan; National Library of Scotland, Edinburgh; Natural History Museum, London; New Bedford Whaling Museum, Massachusetts; Norfolk Museum, Norfolk; Norsk Polarinstitutt, Tromsø; Nottingham University Library, Nottingham; Scott Polar Institute, Cambridge; Royal Scottish Geographical Society, Glasgow; and the National Archives of Norway, Oslo. I also wish to record my gratitude to Laila Andreassen, for her invaluable editorial advice, and Per Kyrre Reymert for kindly proof-reading the final draft. Lastly, I would like to thank my family, Janette, Philip and Mark, who have not overly complained about my lifelong fascination, or even obsession, with Spitsbergen and its early history.

Sheffield, October 2009
John T. Reilly

Tourist Post

Spitsbergen's early postcards provide a fascinating snapshot of the island's past; artefacts of history frozen in time. More than any other tourist destination, these cards are a unique combination of postal, social and local history. Those with messages can open the door to the daily routine of the pioneer tourists, with their details of sea and weather conditions, social activities, ships' cuisine, or simply the travellers' views of events. Understandably, such ephemera have been keenly sought after by collectors and their careful study of card etiquettes and cachets has meant that it is now often possible to identify the shipping company, or even the particular vessel, from which a card originated. Postcards may also provide supportive evidence for a ship's itinerary, with clarification of dates and locations visited, even to the extent of confirming whether a particular vessel reached Spitsbergen at all. Recently, a card, dated 1st August 1914, was noted to bear the message, "because of the war, we shall have to go straight back to Bremen" a statement that has allowed the final days of "Prinz Friedrich Wilhelm's" cruise to be accounted for. Who can tell what future finds might reveal about the "golden age" of Arctic tourism.

A card advertising the Hagen's Tourist Office, Oscars Plads, Hammerfest (1910). The company, established in 1855, sold postcards, photographs, as well as souvenirs from Spitsbergen, including walrus teeth and polar bear skins, to visiting tourist ships.

The "10 øre" Spitsbergen 'tourist' stamp, printed in 1896.

Cancel applied by the sub-postmaster at the tourist hotel in Adventfjorden in 1896.

The early visitors were inveterate writers who never passed an opportunity of informing family and friends of their daily experiences. Indeed, postcards were one of the few souvenirs that passengers could obtain during their polar cruise and, as a result, many more than one might expect have survived the ravages of time. Cards could be bought on board ship and in various ports *en route*. Haffter, a passenger on the "Auguste Victoria", noted that the number of cards posted during the 1899 cruise came to around 20,000 – an average of fifty cards for each passenger. Indeed, one tourist on the "Kong Harald" posted a record one hundred and two cards in a single day in 1898. It was not uncommon to run out of postage stamps, as did a small post office in northern Norway when six thousand cards were delivered from the "Blücher" in 1904. It was as a direct result of this increasing tourist pressure that led eventually to the Norwegian authorities establishing a regulated and permanent postal service on the island.

Spitsbergen's postal history, however, predates the tourist era, with mail, usually written by expedition members, or Scandinavian hunters, being sent south to the mainland on any obliging vessel. Such letters were only franked once they reached one of the many settlements along the Norwegian coast. Mail from this period is obviously rare and can only be recognised if the author's handwriting can be identified, or if there are clues in the text indicating that the sender was residing in the far north. The situation changed in 1896, when the Vesteraalens Dampsskipselskab (Vesteraalens Steamship Company) constructed a hotel in Adventfjorden and began regular summer cruises between Tromsø and Spitsbergen. To serve their passengers, the company issued two unofficial Spitsbergen "tourist" stamps, a brown 10 øre and a red 20 øre, both depicting a hunter and polar bear. All letters and postcards were cancelled with a blue-lilac coloured rubber stamp marked "ADVENT-BAY" and the year "1896". Mail from tourist ships was often stamped with the individual vessel's dated, or undated, cachet, although all mail still

The "Columbia's" cachet, dated 25th July 1896.

The "Auguste Victoria's" cachet, dated 11th July, 1899.

required an official Norwegian stamp before being posted on the mainland. The "Columbia", which visited the islands in 1895, was the first to carry such a cancellation, a special rectangular cachet, to mark its Spitsbergen cruise.

These early stamps were clearly very popular and J.T. Studley, an English big-game hunter, records that he bought a sheet or two as curios and gave them away to his friends' children as souvenirs. It is known that "Kong Harald" sailed from Hammerfest in 1897 with three thousand "Spitsbergen" 10 øre stamps, a number that gives some indication of their demand. Nevertheless, such private stamps had no postal value and were not recognised by the receiving country. Fred Goldberg, an authority on Spitsbergen's philately, writes that the German postal authorities protested strongly against their use, since at that time mail predominantly came from their ships. As a result, the Norwegian postal authorities opened a seasonal, sub-post office in Advent Bay on the 30th July 1897, under the management of Hammerfest. It was called a "brevhus", or letter-house, and was situated in one of the hotel's rooms. The manager, Emil Ellingsen, was appointed to the non-salaried post of sub-postmaster and was provided with a postmark and a sealing press. The island's first post office, however, was only open during the summer months, from 1897 to 1899. A new post office was established in 1906 in Longyear City and operated similarly until 1910, while a further office at Green Harbour existed from 1908–1914.

Postcard for use by tourists on Bade's "Erling Jarl" cruise, 1896.

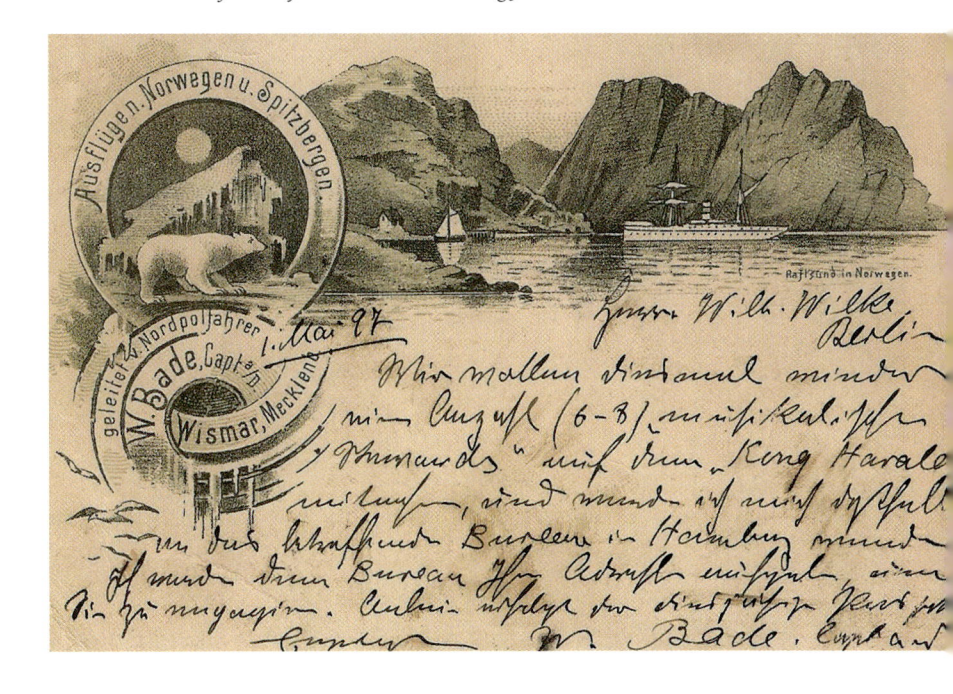

Etiquette commissioned by Captain Bade, 1897.

At the end of the nineteenth century, it was fashionable for tourists to insist on the appropriate cancellation. At towns along the route, passengers would descend on local post offices, forming long queues, whilst harassed postmasters applied stamps and cancellations as fast as possible. On a cruise of the "Auguste Victoria" in 1899, one of the crew acted as "Postmaster", and carried four thousand postcards up the 307-metre summit of Nordkapp so that they could be cancelled on location. Haffter wrote, "The poor man showed me his hand afterwards and it was full of blisters from the stamping." Several years later, tourists were provided with special cachets and ink containers so that they could stamp their own cards for a nominal sum.

The earliest postcards date from 1896 and include one printed in Germany for Captain Wilhelm Bade's tourists sailing on the "Erling Jarl". This card was embellished with a sketch of the "Raftsund" off the Lofoten islands and edged on the left by Bade's motif. In the following year, two different postcards were published, to accompany the cruise of the "Kong Harald", as well as a thousand tourist stamps, or etiquettes, depicting a hunter on skis beneath the words "Arctische Post". Special cachets, or strikes, were used on Bade's ships with the inscriptions indicating places visited and were applied by the head steward when postcards were handed in by the passengers. As the tourist industry developed, printers such G. Hagens Forlag of Hammerfest and W. B. Bøgh Forlag from Trondheim produced ornately coloured postcards entitled, "Hilsen fra Spitsbergen" (Greetings from Spitsbergen), dating from around 1898.

Views of Spitsbergen by well-known artists, including Hans Beat Wieland, Friedrich Kallmorgen and Karl Paul Themistocles von Eckenbrecher, were also popular. The Swiss painter, Wieland, impressed by the novelty of Andrée's

A souvenir postcard from "Kong Harald's" voyage in 1899, with cachets highlighting visits to "Bjørnøya", "Isfjorden", "North Coast" and "80° North".

"Hilsen fra Spitsbergen", printed by W.B.Bøgh, Trondhjem, 1898.

"Hilsen fra Spitsbergen", by G.Hagens forlag, Hammerfest, 1899.

planned balloon expedition, travelled in 1896 to capture his departure on canvas, as drawing-reporter for the *Leipziger Illustrierte*. Inclement weather, however, delayed the flight until the following year and Wieland was unable to witness the event. Nevertheless, during the voyage he painted many scenes along Spitsbergen's coast, twelve of which were used to illustrate postcards, copyrighted by C. Andelfinger and Company of Munich. Kallmorgen, a German artist from Karlsruhe, visited Spitsbergen in 1898 on the "Auguste Victoria" and produced many sketches around Isfjorden and Adventfjorden, while Themistocles von Eckenbrecher, a Greek-German artist, sailed on the "Oihonna" in 1905.

Postcards illustrated with photographic scenes were produced from around 1900 and provide a valuable record of the Spitsbergen's early history. One of the pioneers in this field was the German, Wilhelm Dreesen, court photographer at Flensburg. He began his career in 1865 and twelve years later turned from studio to landscape photography. Dreesen was particularly active in northern Norway and Spitsbergen in the late 1890s and published small collections of his work in the form of art folders, including *Spitsbergen og Polarhavet*, 1896 and *Erinnerungen an meine Nordlandreise*, 1901, as tourist souvenirs. A number of his works were subsequently issued as postcards.

The most prolific photographers, however, were

Self portrait by the German photographer, Wilhelm Dreesen.

Anders Beer Wilse and Paul Eduard Ritter. Wilse was born in Flekkefjord, in Southern Norway, and emigrated as a young man to America, where he developed his passion for photography. He returned in 1888, after an eventful voyage in which his ship, the "Geiser", collided off Newfoundland with the loss of 105 lives. From 1905–1913 he joined the northern tourist ships as photographer, visiting Nordkapp thirty-six times, as well as working as the Svalbard correspondent for the leading Norwegian newspaper, *Aftenposten*. Although Wilse was contracted to produce illustrations for the shipping company's brochures, he retained the right to sell copies of his work to tourists. He endured many hardships, hauling his weighty camera equipment up mountains throughout Norway, as well as photographing the Lofoten cod fishery from an open rowing boat. The national importance of Wilse's work is reflected in the vast amount of material he left behind, including 135,000 negatives and 40,000 original prints, many of which are housed in the Norwegian Folk Museum. Ritter, in contrast, was born in Mecklenburg, Germany and moved to Bergen around 1902 to work as a lithographer in Grieg's book printing and publishing business. He quickly became an accomplished photographer and travelled widely throughout Norway and Spitsbergen with many of his pictures being published as postcards and in art folders. Following his call to service in the German

Anders Beer Wilse (1865-1949), a leading Norwegian photographer, travelled widely throughout Norway and Spitsbergen.

army in 1914, however, his Scandinavian travels ceased and he later settled in Hamburg.

Passengers on the Hamburg-Amerika-Linie cruises could opt to have a series of picture cards sent to friends and family by the shipping company. These alternatives to conventional postcards were pre-printed for selected locations *en route*, to which was added the latest report, telegraphed from the ship.

Postcards have, without doubt, afforded us a unique insight into the golden age of Spitsbergen cruising; a fascinating commentary on a way of life long since past. It was a short lived era, however, lasting essentially from 1884 to its premature demise in 1914, due to the outbreak of World War I. But who were the first tourists and how did they get to this remotest of destinations? Surprisingly, their story has never been told.

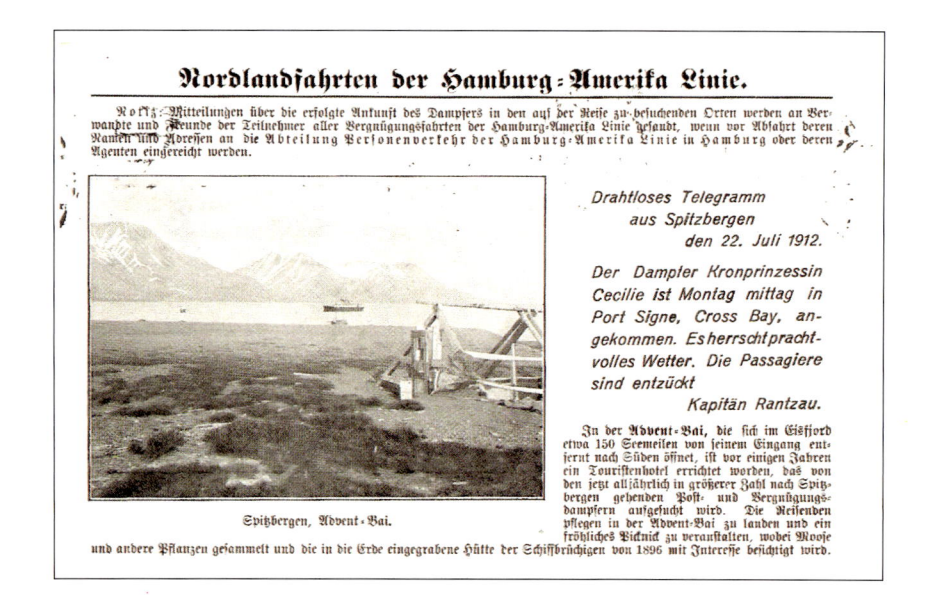

Card with telegraphed report from "Kronprinzessin Cecile", 22nd July, 1912, from Signehamna, Krossfjorden.

Cachets and Postcards

Ships' Cachets

Postcard stamped with "Kong Harald" and "Advent Bay" cachets with 20 øre etiquette, 1912.

Postcard with "Thalia's" cachet and etiquette, dated 15th August 1913, and stamped with cachets recording sites visited.

Hans Beat Wieland (1867–1945)

Adambreen, a small glacier south of Magdalenefjorden.

Grønfjorden, one of Spitsbergen's most fertile areas.

Friedrich Kallmorgan (1856–1924)

A watercolour sketch of Adventfjorden's coastline, from "'Auguste Victoria", July 1898.

"Auguste Victoria" in Bellsund, 1898.

Themistocles von Eckenbrecher (1842–1921)

Nach Norwegen, Spitzbergen u. dem ewigen Eise mit Capt. Bade's Söhne, Wismar i. M.

HORNSUND.

"Hornsund". Eckenbrecher's sketch provides evidence that "Oihonna" visited this remote fjord in 1905.

"Magdalenen-Bay". This small fjord is one of the most beautiful in Spitsbergen and was frequently visited by the early cruise ships.

Wilhelm Dreesen (1839–1926)

"Auf der Bärenjagd" ("On a Bear Hunt"). Many tourists were keen big game hunters and came in search of reindeer, seal, walrus and the most prized trophy of all – polar bear.

"Polareis" ("Pack-ice"). The pack-ice was a popular attraction and the subject of many postcards.

Paul Eduard Ritter (1877–1957)

The Norwegian vessels, "Vega" and "Kong Harald" off Fjortende Julibreen in Krossfjorden, 1912.

Grønfjorden, 1912. The whaling ban in Norwegian waters in 1904 provided the stimulus for the industry's move to Spitsbergen, primarily to Grønfjorden and Bellsund.

The Pioneers

Barto von Löwenigh

The earliest visitors to Spitsbergen were not tourists in today's sense, but were more akin to scientists, hunters and adventurers. The honour of being Spitsbergen's first tourist, therefore, is given to the German, Barto von Löwenigh (1799–1853), an industrialist and burgomaster of Burtscheid, in the Rhineland. In 1827, while travelling in Northern Scandinavia, he encountered Professor Keilhau, a geologist at the University of Oslo. During their stay in Hammerfest, both men determined to visit Spitsbergen, together with two befriended Englishmen. The

The geologist Baltazar Mathias Keilhau (1797–1858) accompanied Löwenigh in 1827.

Title-page of Löwenigh's account of the first tourist trip to Spitsbergen (Courtesy of the National Library of Scotland).

English travelers, however, cried off when they saw the state of the hired sloop and it was left to Keilhau and Löwenigh to make the hazardous voyage northwards. At first, they tried to reach Smeerenburgfjorden, in the hope of encountering Parry's expedition that was on its way home from an unsuccessful attempt on the North Pole, but storms and bad ice conditions drove them off course. Landfall was eventually made at Sørkapp, after which they sailed eastwards reaching Kvalpynten, on the southwest corner of Edgeøya, in early September. Here they found a deserted Russian settlement consisting of several solid-timber buildings, with five crosses nearby,

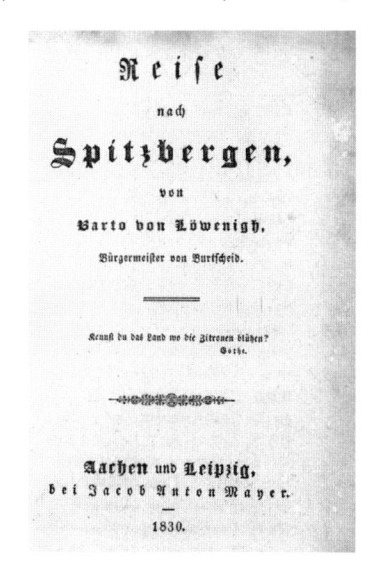

Abandoned Russian hunting settlement on Edgeøya (Keilhau).

furnished with dates and inscriptions. On their return, both men wrote short accounts of their travels, although intriguingly neither mentions the other by name. The importance of their voyage was not just that it resulted in the identification of Pomori, or Russian, settlements on Svalbard's eastern shores, but that it presaged the tourist era.

Du Boulay

Eleven years later, a little known Englishman, John Du Boulay, visited Spitsbergen during the second of two remarkable Grand European tours. In 1836, at the age of 25, he travelled throughout southern Europe before returning home for the winter months. The following year he set out again, travelling alone through Germany, Switzerland, Poland, Russia, Siberia, Sweden and Norway, before ending up in 1838 at the port of Hammerfest. After a week *"of running around"*, he set sail in mid-June for Spitsbergen, but predictably encountered impenetrable ice some distance to the north. His stamina was clearly formidable, for on July 27th 1838 he set out again with a *"fresh captain"*. The following diary entries, although terse and frustratingly short on detail, admirably convey the hardships and stoicism of this remarkable pioneer:

"August 17th. – Rowed in a boat to Foegel Hook in Forland Sound. Landed and pitched a tent. Towards night very cold. I took four men and a boat, with provisions, and arranged with the captain to meet me there as soon as the wind sprung up … Rowed across two or three miles to another spit of land … landed could not sleep.

August 19th. – No vessel in sight. Did not know what had become of it … hard up for food. Shot four gulls, ate them. … made an enormous fire to keep ourselves warm … had no provisions left as had expected vessel on 18th.

August 21st. – Rowed about looking for my ship. Could not see it …

August 23rd. – A sail in view but not our ship … towards night saw again a sail afar off. Very little food indeed left. We determined to row for the sail … Went on board and enquired why it had left us for seven days, and discovered as follows–

After I had left the ship the captain broke into the spirit room and got drunk. He then swore he would go straight back to Norway, and started, leaving the four men and myself on Spitsbergen. Fortunately, however, the remainder of the crew went in a body and said they insisted on his keeping his engagement, so he had to turn round and make for the Foreland Hook, where we had landed. Adverse winds, however, kept him back, and so we were left for seven days with only one day's provisions, and must have died of hunger had I not fortunately met with a seal."

Unperturbed by his ordeal, Du Boulay successfully persuaded the skipper to head further north:

"*August 25th and 26th. – Tried to see how far north I could go … very nearly touched 80°. Here I found ice stretching everywhere, so had to turn back, and ran into Magalena Bay, where I anchored.*

August 27th. – Rowed out seven hours in a small boat … and explored Cross Bay … Picked up a piece of coal … took a walk between glaciers and the shore which is full of most beautiful transparent ice caverns."

Following his return to England, Du Boulay settled down to family life at Donhead Hall, amidst rural Wiltshire, and spent his remaining years in relative obscurity. Fortunately, more than half a century later, he published his diary, under the quaint title *Travels through Spitzbergen, Siberia, Russia, &c., and around the seven churches in Asia Minor*, so preserving his improbable exploits for posterity.

Yachting Sportsmen

During the later half of the nineteenth century, many tourists and sportsmen ventured to Spitsbergen in their own yachts. It was, however, the 31-year old Marquess of Dufferin and

Marquess of Dufferin and Ava (1826–1902).

Ava, then Lord Dufferin, who set the example in 1856 when he voyaged northwards in his flimsy-hulled yacht "Foam". He visited Iceland, Jan Mayen and after cruising the Greenland Sea for eleven days reached the west coast of Spitsbergen. The "Foam" eventually reached the safety of Engelsbukta, where Dufferin, moved by the desolation of his surroundings, wrote: "*...its most striking feature was the stillness, and deadness, and impassibility of this new world: ice, and rock, and water surround us; not a sound of any kind interrupted the silence; the sea did not break upon the shore; no bird or any living thing was visible; the midnight sun, by this time muffled in a transparent mist, shed an awful lustre on glacier and mountain; no atom of vegetation gave token of the earth's vitality; an universal numbness and dumbness seemed to pervade the solitude. I suppose in scarcely any other part of the world is this appearance of deadness so strikingly exhibited.*" In contrast, he found the unique, haze-free quality of the arctic light a poetic experience: "*The belt of unclouded atmosphere was etherealised to an indescribable transparency, and up into it there gradually grew – above the starboard ice – a forest of thin, lilac peaks, so faint, so pale, that had it not been for the gem-like distinctness of their outline, one could have deemed them as unsubstantial as the spires of fairy-land.*" His party en-

The "Foam" beset in ice south of Bjørnøya, which thwarted Dufferin's attempts at landing.

34

countered several exposed coffins belonging to the whaling era but apparently not enough deer to satisfy their hunting desires. Nevertheless, a polar bear was shot and: "… *so gloriously crowned our visit to Spitzbergen, that our disappointment about the deer was no longer thought of; it was therefore with light hearts, and most complete satisfaction, that we prepared for our departure.*"

A few years later, James Lamont began a series of expeditions to Spitsbergen, firstly in the "Genevra" and later in the "Diana". His main interest was hunting, to which he devoted much of his time, favouring the eastern areas, including Storfjorden, Edgeøya and the adjacent islands. We are indebited to Lamont for some of the best observations on the island's flora and fauna and for two delightful volumes of sport, adventure and reflection. Lamont's legacy also includes the discovery of coal in Adventfjorden, an observation that led to the mining industry of today, and the correct chart positioning of the island of Hopen. The Englishmen, Alfred Newton, a leading ornithologist, and Edward Birkbeck visited Spitsbergen in the "Sultana" in 1864 to record (or shoot!) the bird species along the west coast. Leigh Smith made a number of visits between 1871 and 1880 and helped map the eastern extremity of Nordaustlandet, while Sir Henry Gore-Booth, in the "Lancashire Witch", managed to reach the island's Nordkapp in 1888. In the same year, Walter Clutterbuck, chartered the whaling barkentine "Traveller" and visited Smeerenburgfjorden and Isfjorden as part of a five month

Coal deposits were discovered by the crew of "Diana" in Adventfjorden in 1871.

Birds shot by Walter Clutterbuck, 1888.

sporting trip. His views of game-hunting typified the Victorian ambivalence towards the activity. He lamented, for example, the shooting of a defenceless bear as not being worthy of "sport" and yet wrote of his slaughter of small waders: "*It was not in the least shy of strangers. When it was washing itself in a small brook, or digging about for provisions, you could walk right up; and if you shot its sister dead at its side, this bird did not care two straws, but just gave a bit of a flutter with its wings and went on pecking about as if nothing had happened, waiting patiently till its turn came. In fact, this was a most satisfactory bird, and I repeat that we wished there were more of them.*"

In 1898, Major Andrew Coats, a member of the wealthy Paisley thread-making family, undertook a sporting trip to Novaya Zemlya and the east coast of Spitsbergen, in his steam-yacht "Blencathra". He was accompanied by the Scottish explorer, William Spiers Bruce, and although the heavy pack-ice thwarted their sporting plans, the voyage proved to be most useful to Bruce. It introduced him, not only

Andrew Coats on the main deck of the "Blencathra" (Courtesy of the Glasgow Digital Library).

36

"Blencathra" in the pack-ice off Novaya Zemyla 1898.

to the Coats family who would help finance his National Scottish Antarctic Expedition (1902–1904), but also to Spitsbergen's research opportunities. Indeed, Bruce visited Spitsbergen, as well as Prins Karls Forland, many times over the following decade and become an acknowledged authority on the region. Finally, Colonel Henry Feilden, an expert on arctic botany, undertook studies in 1894 along the western coast of Spitsbergen in his yacht "Saida".

The era of the "Gentleman Yachtsman" was not restricted to the British. Prinz Heinrich von Bourbon of Austria visited Spitsbergen in "Fleur-de-Lys I" in 1891 and "Fleur-de-Lys II" in 1892. Surveys were undertaken of sever-

Colonel Henry Feilden (1838–1921), British Army Officer, amateur naturalist and President of Norwich Naturalist's Society, visited Spitsbergen in 1894 (Courtesy of Norfolk Museum).

37

Marsh Saxifrage (Saxifraga hirculus L.), a common arctic species. Collected by Henry Feilden, Adventfjorden, 1–2nd July 1894 (Courtesy of Norfolk Museum).

al anchorages and the resultant charts, although adopted by the Admiralty in 1899, were subsequently shown to be inaccurate. His wife, Aldegonda, Princess of Braganza (Portugal), joined him on the 1892 cruise, during which she noticed a little known bay at the eastern end of Van Mijenfjorden. Her description led to the inlet being named Braganzavågen in her honour. Finally, in 1898 a member of the Italian aristocracy sailed to Spitsbergen in the yacht "Jela", during which hunting parties visited Danskøya and Amsterdamøya.

Henry Clodius

The first "true" Spitsbergen tourist cruise, however, was organised by the Norwegian opportunist Henry D. Clodius in 1881. He chartered the "Pallas", a 507-ton vessel, and placed advertisements in European hunting magazines, including the *Field*, promising participants unrivalled opportunities for polar bear, seal, reindeer and walrus hunting as well as unlimited fowling. Clodius recruited the assistance of the veteran arctic skipper, Elling Carlsen, and undoubtedly his presence on board was a great reassurance to all. The trip was advertised at twenty pounds per person for the scheduled 14 days cruising and hunting in Spitsbergen waters. The financial viability of the venture was in doubt from the outset, however, as fewer than the required sixty participants had signed up. In the end, the party comprised 28 English tourists, 21 men and 7 women, with the remainder coming from Germany and Scandinavia. Those on board included field naturalists, big-game hunters, yachting enthusiasts and sight-seers. A taxidermist was also on hand, whose job it was to preserve the eagerly anticipated trophies.

The "Pallas" departed from Bergen, after a delay of several days, during which Clodius attempted to improve the expedition's finances by agreeing to transport freight to Tromsø. The vessel finally left Norway with two whale boats and their crews on board and having had a crow's nest fitted to the fore-top mast. Several ladies had brought fishing tackle and caught cod from the ship's side, while the shooters "dropped" a few birds into the sea. The entrances to Hornsund and Bellsund were judged to be impassable by the ice-pilots and the "Pallas" finally anchored in Grønfjorden, where the sportsmen spent twenty-two hours ashore in parties of four, hunting reindeer and geese. The sport was clearly not demanding, as according to Abel Chapman, *"the reindeer were very fearless, and took little or no notice of the report of a rifle. They probably mistook it for the sounds caused by the cracking and slitting of the glaciers, noises which ceaselessly reverberated around. One of our party fired eight or nine shots at four bucks, and when one or two of them fell, the others coolly walked up and began sniffing curiously at the bodies of their late companions."*

The cruise then proceeded north to Magdalenefjorden where they encountered the Norwegian whaling schooner "Hvitfisken", with a full cargo of two hundred and fifty white whales, seals, eiderdown and two polar bears that had been shot in Bellsund. According to Chapman, *"the little vessel lay islanded among the floating skins of her prey, and surrounded by a struggling crowd of fulmars, which quarrelled and fought over the blubber, most audaciously regardless of our presence within a few feet."* They proceeded north again, past the west side of Danskøya, and were finally stopped by a field of unbroken

Elling Carlsen (1819–1900), ice-master on the "Pallas", was best known for the first circumnavigation of Spitsbergen in 1863 and Novaya Zemyla in 1871. He was also a member of the Austrian Polar Expedition 1872–74 that discovered Franz Josef Land.

ice at 79° 55°N. The "Pallas" then turned south and returned to Bergen eight days later.

Several tourists become increasingly disillusioned during the cruise, as the fourteen scheduled days in Spitsbergen had been reduced to just over a week. The captain's decision to turn back, in order to save money, had resulted in a heated argument in Grønfjorden and it had even been proposed to throw Clodius overboard. At Tromsø, twelve of the tourists took out an advertisement in a local newspaper criticising the facilities onboard and the false expectations they were given for the possibilities of fishing and hunting. Finally, the price of the tour was suddenly doubled, leading Wolley to describe the whole adventure as a "Spitsbergen Swindle". Clodius never organised another trip and later emigrated to America.

Three passengers, Alfred Cocks, Abel Chapman and Phillipps Wolley, despite the limited time ashore, were still able to make and publish important observations on the island's natural history. Chapman and Cocks, for example, documented twenty-one species of bird, including several that were firsts for the islands. Chapman, although a "big-game hunter", paradoxically went on to establish several important National Parks including the Kruger National Park in South Africa and the Coto Doana National Reserve in southern Spain.

English Cruises

In the 1880's, the Orient Steam Navigation Company was forced to consider alternative employment for its ageing fleet of ships, particularly during the "off peak" periods of its seasonal Australian trade. The solution was the innovative concept of the "holiday cruise", a venture that took advantage of Europe's economic progress and the increase in middle class income and leisure time. Although an untested concept, it did build upon the organised group holiday that had been popularised in the 1860's by travel agents, such as Thomas Cook & Sons. In addition, the chance to follow in the wake of the "well-heeled" and the belief in the medicinal properties of "sea air" provided added appeal. The Orient Line's earliest endeavours took place in 1884, when the passenger steamer "Ceylon" undertook three cruises, including one to Norway and Spitsbergen. Sadly, little is known of this pioneering polar cruise, other than that the "Ceylon" departed from Tromsø in mid-July with eighty tourists. It may be sur-

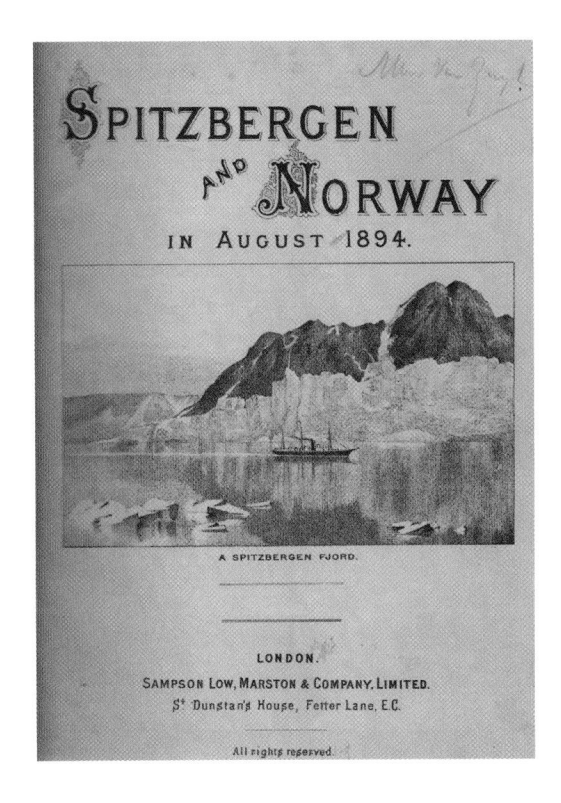

A quality tour guide, written by George Temple, R.N., for passengers on the 1894 cruise. It was through such attention to detail that Orient Steam Navigation Company established an international reputation for pleasure cruising.

Brochure advertising "Lusitania's" schedule from London to Spitsbergen, 1894.

mised, however, that the cruise was not an overwhelming success, as a decade was to pass before the company returned to Spitsbergen in the "Lusitania".

The talus formations of Templet described by Victor Gatty (1894) as "cliffs of a peculiar formation, common in Spitsbergen, but which I have never come across elsewhere … tiers of conical-shaped barrels, ranged one upon the other".

Lusitania

The "Lusitania" departed from London in August 1894, in what the company's brochures described as a "thirty-three day pleasure cruise". Calls were made at Leith and Tromsø, before she headed north to Spitsbergen and the pack-ice at around 80° North. Victor Gatty, an English businessman and alpinist, noted that the arrival in Sassenfjorden was celebrated in true British fashion with a game of cricket on

"Lusitania" at 80° 30'N by the artist Tristram Ellis (1894).

The "Garonne's" dinner menu, 5th August, 1896, Adventfjorden. Passengers were offered the choice of boiled turbot, ox-tail, roast pork and apple sauce, roast chicken and bread sauce, or boiled neck of mutton (courtesy of the Bodleian Library, Oxford).

deck, whilst *"the midnight sun gilded the snowy peaks at the head of the fjord"*. Alfred Shaw, one of the best slow bowlers in England and past captain of Nottinghamshire contributed to the bowling attack. Next morning, Gatty went ashore and climbed a flat-topped hill at the mouth of Sassendalen, which he named Ptarmigan Hill (Skarvrypehøgda). From the summit, he obtained wonderful views of Templet, rising precipitously from the sea. The wild panoramic scenes clearly inspired him for the following day he set out to explore the peaks to the south, one of which was named Lusitaniafjellet. The "Lusitania" returned to Spitsbergen in 1895 and was subsequently employed on the Liverpool-Halifax-St John service before being wrecked in 1901 on Cape Race.

Garonne

The Orient Line offered a similar itinerary in 1896, with the added attraction of observing *en route* an eclipse of the sun. Crucially, there had been no total eclipse of the sun visible in Britain since 1715 and so the event of August 1896 provided a unique opportunity for tourists to witness this natural phenomenon. The "Garonne", a sister ship to the "Lusitania", had pioneered cruises to the Norwegian fjords and Scandinavian capitals since 1889. Ninety-two passengers signed up for the 50 guinea cruise including, for the second time, the watercolour artist Tristram Ellis. Also on board was Norman Lockyer, an expert in astronomy, who gave lectures and arranged practical classes explaining the nature of the midnight sun and solar eclipses and who planned to undertake further scientific investigations during the voyage. The "Garonne" set out from the Thames and reached the northern port of Vadsø early in August, in plenty of time to observe the solar event. In the end, however, fog prevented any sighting at Vadsø, although only a few miles away, the eclipse was seen in all its splendour and the "obscuring moon was surrounded by a corona that measured half its own apparent diameter".

Once anchored in Adventfjorden, many passengers sought game ashore. Some were clearly well equipped, as Studley, a big-game hunter attached to Martin Conway's expedition, noted: "*one Frenchman came ashore armed to the teeth. In his hand was a revolver, at his side a long couteau de chasse, and on his shoulder a combination double-barrelled rifle and shot-gun. After remaining on the beach for twenty minutes he fired off all the barrels of his revolver into the air, then peacefully rejoined the steamer.*" Conway's expedition rations could not compete with "Garonne's" cuisine and Studley did not hesitate to join a number of tourist friends for a lavish evening diner of boiled turbot, roast pork, chicken and mutton, on board ship. The "Garonne" returned to Spitsbergen the following year for the last time, after which she was sold to a Seattle based company, for use during the Alaskan gold rush, and was eventually broken up in 1905.

Ophir

The "Ophir", one of the best known Mail Liners on the Suez Canal route to Australia, first visited Spitsbergen in 1899. Amongst her passengers was W. L. Brown, a gentleman who typified the Victorian enthusiasm for documenting and cataloguing the natural world. He obtained seawater samples throughout the voyage and with the help of a microscope recorded the type and abundance of the various phytoplankton. Indeed, his crude pencil notes, archived in London's Natural History Museum, remain one of the few tangible records of this early cruise.

The 6,910 ton, "Ophir", visited Spitsbergen in 1899, 1903 and 1904.

English cruises were curtailed in 1901 and 1902 due to the high freight charges associated with the Boer War and the chartering of some Orient vessels to the British Government. As a result, the "Ophir" did not to return to Spitsbergen until 1903, although it was the 1904 cruise which was to play an unexpectedly important role in Spitsbergen's early history. On aboard, was the Rector of Goldhangar, the Reverend Frederick Gardner and his elder daughter. Gardner was one of the last "gentleman" rectors, in that he came from a middle class family and was sufficiently well off to be able to pursue his interest in travel. He was appointed at the age of twenty-nine and subsequently became good friends with the local doctor, J. Salter and a mining engineer and prospector, Ernest Mansfield. Both men were widely travelled. Salter, for example, was an ardent big game-hunter and possessed many hunt-

"Ophir's" crew, 1904.

Reverend Frederick Gardner (1864–1936) first visited Spitsbergen in 1904. His mineral prospecting in Recherchefjorden encouraged further visits and led to the establishment of the Northern Exploration Company.

The Rectory in Goldhangar where Frederick Gardner, Ernest Mansfield and J. Salter met in 1904.

Ernest Mansfield (1862–1924), hunter, prospector, author and entrepreneur. Mansfield encouraged Gardner to visit Spitsbergen in 1904 and subsequently became a key player in the island's early industrialization.

ing trophies from his time in Siberia and Northern Russia, while Mansfield had prospected for minerals worldwide. Listening to his friends' romanticised tales, Gardner became excited at the idea of finding gold and decided to use the opportunity of his planned cruise to Spitsbergen to pursue this idea.

The "Ophir's" tourists pose for the camera, Recherchefjorden 26th July, 1904.

The "Admiralen" in Recherchefjorden, 1904. A converted freighter with specially fitted cookers, she was an experimental prototype for the "whaling factory ship". Her success in Spitsbergen's waters contributed to the opening up of the Antarctic whale fishery.

The 103-ton whale catcher "Ørnen" was built in 1902 in Sandefjord. She commenced whaling in Spitsbergen and Bjørnøya in 1903, although her most successful season was in 1904 working alongside "Admiralen". She relocated to the Antarctic fishery in 1905 due to increasing competition in the Spitsbergen area.

A whale catcher's harpoon in Spitsbergen's waters. Designed by Svend Foyn, a Norwegian seaman, after many years of trial and error.

The "Ophir" set sail with one hundred and ninety-one passengers, mostly from England, but with a small number from Belgium, Australia and America. Two days later, a Norwegian pilot was taken on board, to help navigate the tortuous waters of the "Inner Lead", and a representative from Thomas Cook & Sons, who would act as tour guide for the cruise. At Recherchefjorden, passengers had the opportunity to view a glacier at close hand, scramble along the shoreline, or explore the, "*subtle scents of a derelict whale carcass.*" Nearby, the 1,517-ton Norwegian factory ship "Admiralen" lay at anchor and her crew invited "Ophir's" tourists to witness the processing of several whales.

In Recherchefjorden, Gardner undertook his amateur prospecting activities. One evening, after his fellow passengers had returned for supper, he remained ashore and spent the night collecting pieces of rock and samples of shingle. The products of this unusual nocturnal activity were carefully stowed onboard next morning and brought back to England for his friends' scrutiny. The samples' gold content was confirmed and the findings so encouraged Gardner and Mansfield that they returned to Spitsbergen the following summer. Subsequent activities led to the establishment of the Northern Exploration Company which played an important role in Spitsbergen's early industrialization.

Garonne's distinguished Passengers (1896)

William Morris

William Morris was the most influential and famous "bookman" of his age, being not only a writer of original verse and prose, but also a translator, calligrapher, collector and publisher. Morris had some significant warnings of declining health and his physician suggested that he may benefit from a cruise in the "Garonne" to Norway. The trip was not a success as he was weary and depressed and too weak to undertake any of the inland excursions. He also suffered from hallucinations. Coils of rope lying on the deck, "… appeared to his disordered mind like a great serpent preparing to crush the life out of him." Morris did not venture as far as Spitsbergen, but was left ashore at Vadsø until the "Garonne" picked him up on its return voyage. He died several months later.

William Morris (1834–1896)

Sir Norman Lockyer

Lockyer was a British astronomer and well known scientist of his day. He founded the prestigious scientific journal *Nature* and served as editor for over fifty years. He is remembered chiefly for his contributions to astrophysics and proposed that a prominent yellow spectral line taken from the sun during a solar eclipse was due to an hypothetical element to which he gave the name "Helium". He is also remembered for his astronomical interpretations of ancient and prehistoric sites and, as a result, has been called the "father of archaeoastronomy".

Sir Norman Lockyer (1836–1920)

Cuzco

The "Cuzco" undertook her only high latitude cruise in 1900, visiting Norway, Spitsbergen and Iceland. Unusually heavy pack ice was encountered and forced a risky anchoring off Torrellbreen, before the safety of Recherchefjorden was reached. Unfortunately, the lateness of the season was marked by an exceptionally extensive snow cover and the shore party had to trudge through deep coastal slush to reach Renardbreen, a popular tourist attraction. The following day, the more resilient travellers were towed in an open boat to view Recherchebreen's snout. The tour then returned home via Iceland and the Faeroe Islands, where a scheduled landing was abandoned due to an outbreak of measles.

The 3,900-ton "Cuzco" visited Norway, Spitsbergen and Iceland in 1900.

Mexico

In 1902 Orient Line's "Mexico" departed from Tilbury with a 114 passengers. Despite coastal ice preventing entry to Recherchefjorden, her passengers were rewarded with a sighting of a polar bear, a rare event along the island's west coast. The artist, Tristram Ellis, described the encounter; *"the bear rose up and seemed uncertain of his course of action, sniffed the air, evidently trying to discover what peculiar sort of animal the ship was, and ran up and down the ice, picking his way over the broken pieces. At last the Captain blew the siren, and our friend stood transfixed with astonishment, then with one backward look he started on his masterly retreat towards the East Glacier, stumbling over a mile or more of broken ice on his way to the open water, and swam for the shore."* Ellis clearly found the arctic scenery inspirational and his four visits to Spitsbergen on the "Lusitania" (1894), "Garonne" (1897), "Mexico" (1902) and "Ophir" (1904), resulted in a significant number of paintings and sketches.

Route of the "Mexico", 1902.

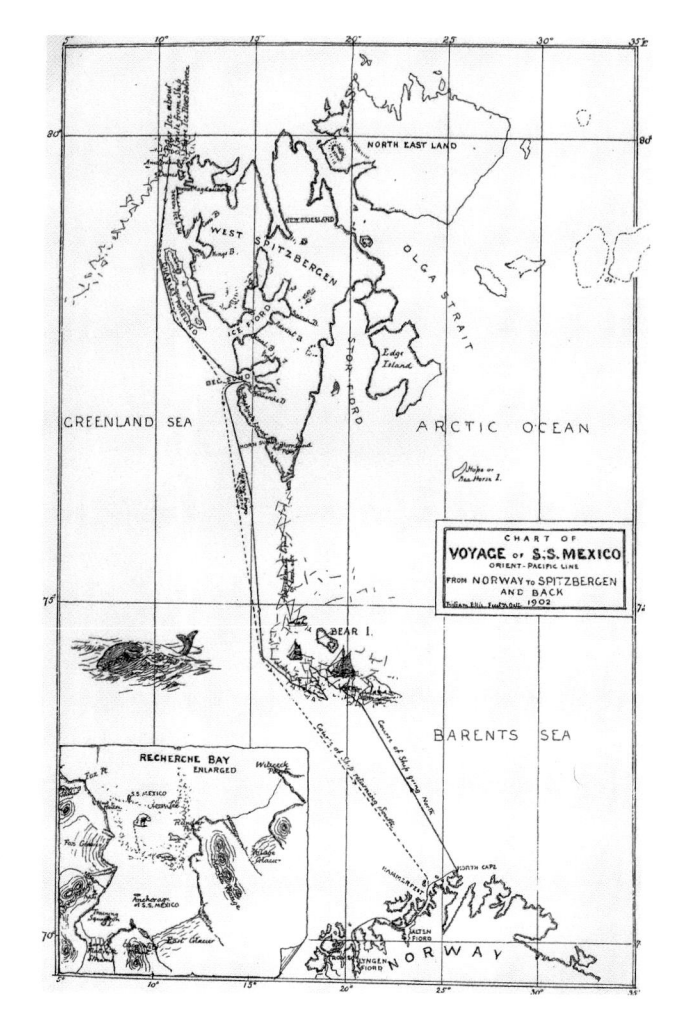

Sketch of polar bear in Recherchefjorden by Tristram Ellis, 1902.

Vectis

William L. Wyllie (1851–1931), marine artist and etcher, who accompanied his wife on the 1906 and 1907 "Vectis's" cruises.

The only P&O vessel to visit Spitsbergen was the "Vectis", which visited the islands annually between 1905 and 1912. She was built in 1881 as the "Rome" and converted to a First Class only cruising yacht when her line voyage carrying was over. The fittings were lavish and included electric lighting and running hot and cold water. Smoking rooms, music and recreational salons and dark rooms for photography were added, while a fully qualified medical officer and a group of musicians accompanied the voyage. Cruises lasted twenty eight days with fares starting at thirty guineas. The author, M.A. Wyllie, accompanied her

Poster painted by W. L. Wyllie advertising P&O cruises to Norway and Spitsbergen in the "Vectis" (Courtesy of the Greenwich Maritime Museum).

58

Graves of Norwegian whalers, Recherchefjorden, by W. L.Wyllie 1906 (Courtesy of Greenwich Maritime Museum).

husband, the marine artist William L. Wyllie, on the 1906 cruise. She wrote a travelogue of the voyage, *Norway and its Fjords, 1907*, which contains an evocative account of the whale fishery, which had moved to Spitsbergen's waters several years previously; "*We pulled away past the steamer to a barque of about 700 tons, astern of which were four carcasses of whales. The harpoon was still sticking in the flesh of one of them, and from it a stream of blood oozed, staining the water crimson. Here again the fulmar fought and jostled, snapping in the greasy mixture. As we approached the ladder, we noticed that the whole of the waterline of the barque was thickly coated with a layer of grease. The steps were also covered, and the hand-rope felt almost like a tallow-dip. The decks were black and all the poop lumbered with oil barrels. Just abaft the mast were the great cauldrons into which a strange engine, not unlike a mud-dredger in shape, poured a continuous stream of blubber, cut into lumps about a foot square. A hot, greasy smell pervaded everything. Just at this moment the gory carcass of a whale, from which the head, tail, fins and every scrap of fat had been cut, was cast adrift, and floated away, the centre of a screaming cloud of fulmars.*"

In 1907, the ice remained very much further south than usual and the "Vectis" was only able to reach 74° 30'N, midway between Nordkapp and Spitsbergen. William Wyllie, once again a passenger onboard, wrote, "*Every now and then the fog closed round the ship, accentuating the noise made by the ice-floes as they floated passed, grinding and crashing against each other. The captain, first and second officer and the pilots were on the bridge, and right in the bow stood the third officer with a megaphone, through which he shouted, 'Ice on the port bow, Sir!', or 'Ice to starboard!' as the case happened to be. One floe battering against the ship was quite sufficient to show what might happen had the captain not used all his skill to prevent accidents.*"

Whalers in Recherchefjorden by W. L. Wyllie, 1906 (Courtesy of the New Bedford Whaling Museum).

A souvenir photograph of the "Vectis" off Norway 1908, that was signed by the Commander and his crew.

A passenger's photograph album depicting life on board the "Vectis", 1910.

Tourists scrambling on and around Renardbreen, Recherchefjorden, 1910.

Watercolour of Arctic skua by W. L. Wyllie (Courtesy of Greenwich Maritime Museum).

Watercolour of Arctic tern and sextant by W. L. Wyllie (Courtesy of Greenwich Maritime Museum). While anchored in Recherchefjorden, the crew of the "Vectis" embarked on a shooting trip to Akseløya, a strange 8.5 kilometre long island at the entrance to Van Mijenfjorden. Remains of a hunting camp were found, including a crude, but functional, sextant made from oak. Carcasses of birds were also brought back which, together with the sextant, provided still life compositions for the evening art classes.

Drawing of "Vectis" blocked by ice at 74 degrees longitude, 1907, by W. L. Wyllie (Courtesy of Greenwich Maritime Museum).

Wilhelm Bade's Cruises

Despite the Orient Line being first to visit Spitsbergen, the "father" of polar tourism was undoubtedly Captain Eduard Wilhelm Bade, a German naval officer from the town of Wismar in Mecklenburg. Bade gained his first arctic experience at fifteen, but his greatest adventure was as second officer of the "Hansa", a small schooner that accompanied the "Germania" on an abortive attempt to reach the North Pole in 1869. The expedition leader ill-advisedly tried to force a passage northwards, along Greenland's east coast, against the powerful polar current. The "Hansa" was soon beset and crushed by the ice, with her crew being forced to take refuge on an ice-flow. The men spent a miserable winter, drifting southwards for 237 days in a shelter made from salvaged coal blocks. At last they were able to take to their boats and eventually rowed around Cape Farewell to meet a Danish ship which took them back to Europe.

Undaunted, Bade returned to the arctic on various sealing expeditions, although little is known of this period in his life. Indeed, it is possible that he may have taken a small party of fellow-countrymen on a cruise from Norway to Spitsbergen as early as 1871.

Early cruises (1891–1895)

German interest in the North, apart from the region's obvious political and economic impor-

Captain Wilhelm Bade (1843–1903), the father of polar tourism.

Max Zeppelin's account of the 1892 cruise of the "Amely".

tance, had been kindled by the exploits of their Emperor, William II. He loved all things Norwegian and spent the summer months, between 1889 and 1914, cruising the fjords in his yacht "Meteor". Furthermore, the development of the luxury cruise ship gave the opportunity for "well-to-do" Germans to travel in style and to follow in their Emperor's footsteps. Both these factors helped fuel the German love of the arctic, an enthusiasm that continues unabated today. Bade appreciated the business potential of this interest and in 1891 organised the "Württemberg Spitzbergen Expedition", the first of a series of arctic cruises. The steamer "Amely", chartered from a German deep-sea fishing company, set sail from Tromsø with a small band of game-hunters and prospectors. The party got off to a flying start, with many seals being taken off Bjørnøya, before they landed on the island's southern shore, during unusually clement weather. They then visited Bellsund, Isfjorden, Magdalenefjorden and eventually stopped at 80° N. Interestingly, Max Zeppelin, who had joined the cruise to evaluate the island's coal deposits, concluded that mining on Spitsbergen would not be economical.

These experiences led Bade to believe in Stefansson's concept of the "friendly arctic" and to the conclusion that the northern lands could not only sustain its human inhabitants, but also provide profit for the non-native entrepreneur. In 1892, he co-founded the "Nordische Hochsee-fischerei Gesellschaft" (Nordic Sea Fisheries Company) in Mülheim an der Ruhr, in Germany's industrial heartland. Arctic tourism and coal mining, as well as whaling, were the business's core activities and the enterprise received the backing of a number of leading German industrialists.

Although the company failed after only one season, Bade continued his arctic tours with a second and larger cruise in 1893. The "Admiral", chartered from the German East African Shipping Company, set out from Lübeck to rendezvous at Tromsø with the German fishing vessel "Glückauf" for the voyage north to Spitsbergen. It is known, from the entries recorded in a guest book at the Norwegian whaling station at Skaarø (modern day "Store Skorøya"), that the majority of tourists were German, while a few heralded from Czechoslovakia and Holland. Passengers were given the unique opportunity of boarding the "Glückauf" and to witness a whale hunt in all its brutality at close quarters. Later, both ships called in at Adventfjorden and Grønfjorden, where a whale caught at sea was presented to two Norwegian hunters who were spending the summer on Spitsbergen. The cruise then headed north, reaching impenetrable pack-ice at 80° N 45', before returning to Lübeck by the end of August.

The success of "Admiral's" cruise encouraged Bade to offer arctic tours on an annual basis, with different chartered vessels. In 1894 he hired the Norddeutscher Lloyd's "Stettin", a 1,815-ton vessel built in 1886 for the Far Eastern Route. The Norwegian skipper, Henrik B. Næss joined the cruise as ice-pilot, to ensure a safe passage in the high north. He typified this hardy band of men, having visited Spitsbergen at the age of eight, crewed many times on arctic sealers as a teenager and qualified as a skipper in his twenties. The following year, Bade chartered the "Stettin's" sister ship, the 1,852-ton "Danzig", for a four week cruise departing in mid-July from Bremerhavn. His son, Axel, joined the tour and in doing so gained the experience that would enable him to lead his own Spitsbergen cruises from 1903, following his father's death. The "Danzig" was not the only German vessel to visit Spitsbergen that year, for the Hamburg-Amerika-

Henrik Næss (1862–1950) was ice-pilot for the tourists ships "Stettin" (1894) and "Garonne" (1896). He is best remembered, however, for being a founder member of the Trondhjem-Spitsbergen Kulkompagni (1900), which helped ensure the successful exploitation of Spitsbergen's coal deposits.

Andrée's gas generators being assembled next to Pike's house (Courtesy of the Grenna Museum).

Linie's steamship, "Columbia" made her second visit to Isfjorden as part of a Norwegian tour, and in doing so ushered in the golden era of German arctic cruising.

Erling Jarl (1896)

The following year, Bade chartered the smaller 677-ton "Erling Jarl" from the Nordenfjeldske Dampskibsselskap (Northern Steamship Company), based in Trondheim. At sixty metres in length, she had the advantage of being able to negotiate the narrow Norwegian fjords and skerries, thus offering tourists a more sheltered passage northwards, as well as the opportunity to visit shallower and less frequented anchorages. Fifty-two passengers joined the cruise, with the prospect of encountering the polar pack, witnessing a total eclipse of the sun and visiting Andrée's base camp. Indeed, mainland Europe was anxiously awaiting news of Andrée's audacious attempt on the North Pole by balloon and the opportunity to witness such an historic event would have been a powerful attraction for many. By the time the tour arrived, Andrée had already established his base camp on Danskøya, in a wooden house constructed earlier by the Englishman, Arnold Pike.

Andrée's wooden prefabricated hangar was erected on the shore of Virgohamna in the summer of 1896, adjacent to Arnold Pike's house (built for an eight-man overwintering, 1888–1889).

The "Erling Jarl" departed from Hamburg and reached Danskegattet, the narrow channel separating Danskøya and Amsterdamøya, just before midnight on July 23rd. The ship's siren announced their arrival as they manoeuvred to

Andrée's balloon station, Danskøya. Painting by Hans B. Wieland, 1896 (Private collection).

within a short distance of Andrée's expedition ship, the steel cargo steamer "Virgo". Next day, the tourists went ashore and were given an introduction to the three Swedish balloonists, Andrée, Strindberg and Fraenkel, as well as a tour of Pike's house and the specially constructed balloon hangar. Andrée freely discussed his plans and showed off his equipment, while Bade exchanged letters and brought news from Europe. The Swiss painter, Hans B. Wieland, who had travelled with Bade to record Andrée's departure, made several paintings and sketches of the scene for posterity.

The cruise then headed northwards, reaching a record 81° 32' 8"N, a feat that had been bettered on only two previous occasions: by Nordenskiöld in 1868 and by the American explorer, Charles Hall in 1871. Brief, but pioneering, visits were then made to the remote fjords, Liefdefjorden and Wijdefjorden, the only tour to do so for many decades. Less than forty-eight hours later, they were back in Danskegattet, to find the balloon inflated and the explorers waiting for an improvement in the weather. The small flotilla was joined by the "Express", a Norwegian vessel that had brought a small group of tourists from the hotel in Adventfjorden, and Arnold Pike's vessel "Victoria". Captain Bade, however, was anxious to be heading south, as they had to be at Vadsö on the 9th August to witness the eclipse of the sun. On July 30th the "Erling Jarl's" crew entertained Andrée and his

"Erling Jarl" in the pack-ice. Painting by Hans B. Wieland, 1896 (Private collection).

"Iceberg". Watercolour by Hans B. Wieland, 1896 (Private collection).

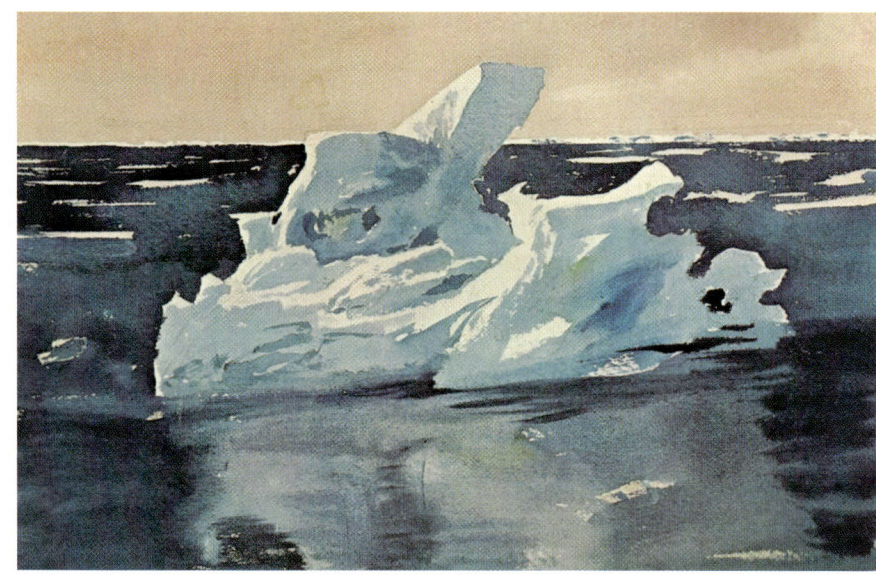

team to a final, sumptuous dinner, that included a concert by the ship's musicians, before they said their farewells. Henri Lachambre, the French designer of Andrée's balloon, described the scene: "… *the crews of the Virgo and Erling Jarl are formed up in a line; at the back, the passengers are grouped round the explorers. Several speeches are made by the captain of the 'Erline Jarl' (sic) and some of the tourists; thereupon a young lady, who is travelling with her fiancé and a relative, attaches to Andrée's arm a blue ribbon, and then hands him for the journey a bottle of the best wine, a cake and a rose-tree with four roses, one for each explorer.*" The "Erling Jarl" then fired off a salvo of twenty-one guns in Andrée's honour and under a heavy sky, headed southwards, visiting Magdalenefjorden, Kongsfjorden, Isfjorden and finally Adventfjorden.

On shore, the tourists met the well-known Swedish scientist, Baron Gerard de Geer, who was attempting to correct inaccuracies in the map of central Spitsbergen. De Geer's party had been taken free of charge to Spitsbergen in Andrée's "Virgo" and then transferred to the "Raftsund", which was bound for Adventfjorden to set up a tourist hotel. Base camp was established at Hotellneset and the party travelled the length and breath of Isfjorden in two small

"Wijde Bay, Spitzbergen". The east coast of Wijdefjorden by Hans B. Wieland, completed on his return in 1897 (Private collection).

A sketch by Hans B. Wieland of the Norwegian hunters' overwintering shelter, Adventfjorden.

Gerard De Geer (1858–1943), geologist and cartographer who met "Erling Jarl's" tourists while mapping Isfjorden, during the summer of 1896 (Alfred J:son Dahllöf. Courtesy of the Royal Library, National Library of Sweden, KoB Alb. 24:55).

boats, returning every two weeks for provisions that had been brought by the Norwegian tourist vessel "Lofoten". De Geer's two months of field work resulted in the most detailed map that had ever been produced of such a large area within the arctic. Nearby, the tourists were also introduced to Sir Martin Conway, an English explorer whose expedition had just returned from making the first crossing of Spitsbergen. Somewhat cheekily, a number of visitors borrowed the expedition's ponies and held a gymkhana, an event that was followed by a dance at the hotel that lasted into the early hours. The following morning, Bade picked

Sir Martin Conway (1856–1937) undertook the first crossing of Spitsbergen in 1896.

up the Swedish scientists and transported them to Sassenfjorden, before heading back to mainland Europe.

Without doubt, the "Erling Jarl's" 1896 cruise was the most ambitious and successful of all the early tourist trips. Never before had visitors been given the opportunity to meet explorers in the field, to reach such a high latitude, or to visit the island's remotest northern fjords.

Kong Harald

The "Kong Harald" was chartered by Wilhelm Bade from the Nordenfjeldske Dampskibsselskap (Northern Steamship

Company) for his arctic cruises from 1897–1899. The 953-ton vessel was built in 1890 in Geestemünde (now a suburb of Bremerhavn) at the Johann C. Tecklenborg shipyard. She possessed the latest fitments, including beautifully decorated cabins, electric lights, bathrooms, bar, a well stocked library and a music room with piano. Bade also provided specially printed postcards and etiquettes (stamps), as well as a small band for evening entertainment. The four week cruises had similar itineraries to previous years, visiting towns along the Norwegian coast, and with landings on Bjørnøya and at sites along Spitsbergen's west coast.

A first hand account of the 1898 voyage was published by the German satirical novelist and poet, Ernest Hugo Baudissin, who was one of his country's most popular contemporary authors. His decision to join the "Kong Harald" resulted from a chance meeting with Bade, whose charisma and passion for the arctic had a persuasive effect on many individuals. Indeed, Bade was renowned for his public lectures in which he promulgated the concept of a friendly Arctic. The cruise with its sixty-one passengers departed from Hamburg at midday on the 30th July and arrived at the small Norwegian village of Kopervik to be greeted with the

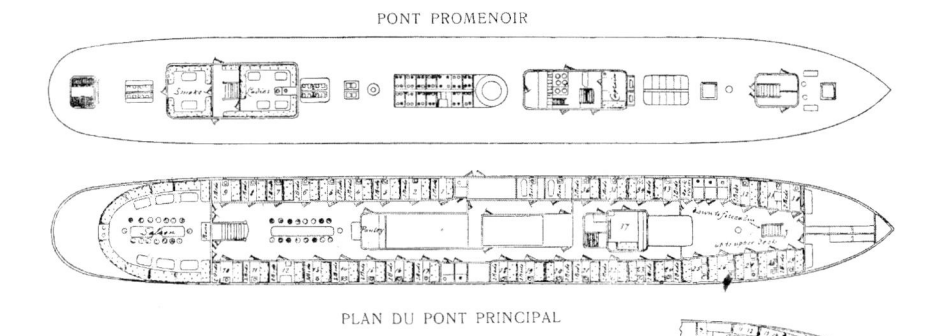

Deck plan of "Kong Harald". Nordensfjeldske Dampskibsselskap brochure, 1906.

news of Bismark's death. Baudisson was struck by the sheer beauty of the Norwegian coastline, especially the precipitous Geirangerfjorden, lined by its patches of cultivated high ground and isolated farmhouses. Nearby, Merok, a scattered village with a post office and several hotels, was noted to be idyllic, but overrun with American and British tourists.

After a tour of Tromsø, the steamer made a brief, but popular, visit to the whaling station at Skaarø, situated some

The German author Ernest Baudissin (pseud. Freiherr von Schlicht) joined the "Kong Harald" cruise in 1898.

fifty miles to the north. Here, during the summer months, up to thirty workers were employed in rendering the whale carcasses to produce oil, meat, bone meal and baleen. Despite arriving on a Sunday, the 1898 tour was greeted by a fully operational plant, with six whales lying along the shore and a fully manned whaler servicing its harpoon equipment. The stench was nauseating and Baudissin records his relief at leaving the area and reaching Hammerfest, the northernmost city in Europe. Skaarö, despite its remoteness, would have been familiar to German tourists, as their emperor, Kaiser Wilhelm II, had previously made a well publicized visit to the site and had witnessed a successful hunt from close quarters. Indeed, the station continued to be a popular tourist attraction up until the 1904 season, when the Norwegian Government introduced a whaling ban in Norwegian waters.

The "Kong Harald" then headed northwards to Bjørnøya where, after a difficult landing in the surf, the more adventurous travellers spent the night ashore exploring the island's coastline. Early next day, they returned aboard, laden with souvenirs that included pebbles, flowering plants and shot sea birds. Visits to Recherchefjorden, Adventfjorden, and Smeerenburgfjorden followed, before the cruise finally

Tourists inspecting the whaling station at Skaarö, 1902.

A "Bade-Flag", designed and sewn by the "Kong Harald's" passengers, 1898.

reached a latitude of 80° 04' N. Herman Klaatsch, professor of anatomy and physical anthropology at Heidelberg, accompanied Baudissin and spent much of his spare time studying the fjords' pelagic fauna. Using Müller nets and a glass lens, he took great delight in showing his fellow travellers the phenomenal wealth of life in the arctic seas. Klaatsch, however, is better remembered for his important and controversial advocacy for the clear division of religion and science, views which changed the way anthropology was subsequently taught.

Special flags, the "Bade-Flags", designed and sewn by the passengers, were flown from the mast of the "Kong Harald", as well as the "Oihonna" during her early cruises. They were based on the schwarz-weiss-rot (black, white, red) German Empire flag with an added walrus motif and a "B" for Bade.

Hertha

Bade was not only a polar explorer but also an ardent hunter, having spent his youth sealing in the high arctic. These passions, coupled with his enthusiasm for developing new tourist opportunities, led to his most ambitious cruise in 1900, when he took a small group of tourists on a hunting trip to the remote waters off Franz Josef Land and along Svalbard's east coast. He chartered the Norwegian sealing bark, "Hertha" of Sandefjord, under Captain Jørgensen, together with a crew of twenty-five.

The voyage was dogged by fog for most of the way and heavy pack ice prevented landings on Franz Josef Land, along the eastern coasts of Kong Karls Land and Hopen. In total, four polar bears and several seals were taken by the party, with the skins being kept as prized "hunting-trophies." The cruise arrived in Hammerfest to be met by the Duke of Abruzzi's expedition ship "Stella Polaris", which had just returned from a year in Franz Josef Land. "Hertha's" tourists were invited on board and became the first to hear that one of her team, Captain Cagni, had reached latitude 86° 34'N, thus beating Nansen's achievement of 1895.

Captain Wilhelm Bade, leader of the 1900 tour to Franz Josef Land and the east coast of Spitsbergen, onboard the "Hertha".

despite attempting to force a route through for twelve days. The "Hertha" then sailed towards the north-east of Svalbard, reaching a northing of 81° 13'N, 38° 30'E, before returning

The 253-ton "Hertha", of the A/S Oceana, Sandefjord, built in 1884 for the pioneer whaler Christian Christensen. She was sunk in 1918 by a German U-boat.

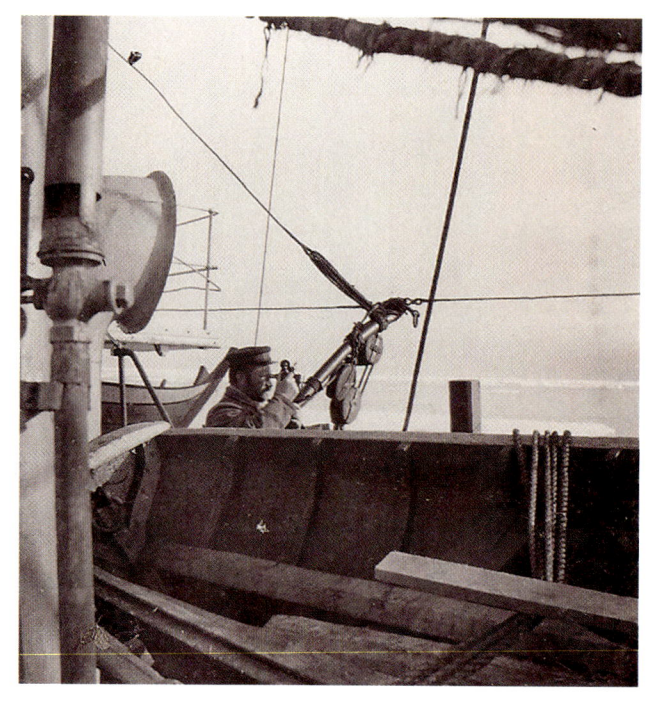

Captain Jørgensen, skipper of the "Hertha" in a lighter moment. In 1898 he led a hunting expedition to Franz Josef Land that resulted in the kill of nearly 300 walruses.

A crew member takes sightings off the southern coast of Franz Josef Land.

Tourists onboard "Hertha" in the pack-ice between Franz Josef Land and Spitsbergen.

A polar bear is spotted on an ice-flow.

One of four bears killed off Spitsbergen's east coast during the 1900 cruise. The skin's were highly prized trophies.

One of many seals taken during the cruise.

The "Stella Polaris" at anchor off Hammerfest, 5th September, 1900. The "Hertha's" tourists were invited aboard and were the first to hear of the expedition's failure to reach the North Pole.

The "Hertha's" tourists relax in Tromsø, where polar skins were traded.

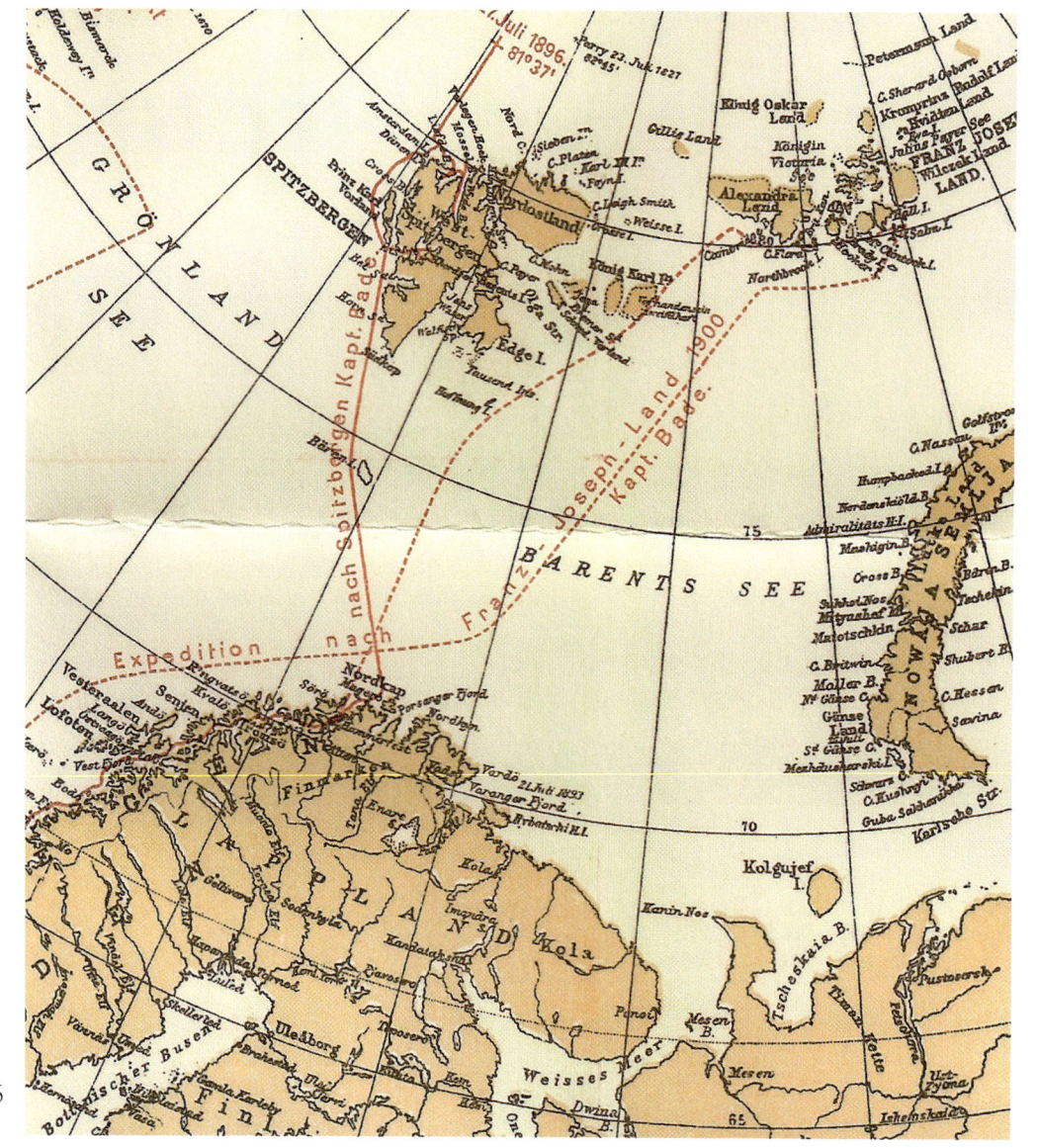

A map detailing the "Hertha's" 1900 route to Franz Josef Land and along Spitsbergen's eastern coast.

A postcard from "Hertha's" 1900 cruise signed by Bade. Note two tourist cachets, the first, "Expedition nach Franz Josef Land", dated 26 August 1900 and a second, "Nordliches Eismeer. 80⁰ Nordbreite", dated 25ᵗʰ August 1900.

Oihonna (1902–1906)

No cruise was organised in 1901, but the following year Bade resumed his activities, hiring the Finnish Steamship Company's ship "Oihonna". The 1072-ton vessel possessed a reinforced hull and was ideally suited for arctic cruising. She visited Spitsbergen twice a year for five consecutive summers, chartered first by Wilhelm Bade in 1902 and then by his son Axel between 1903 and 1906.

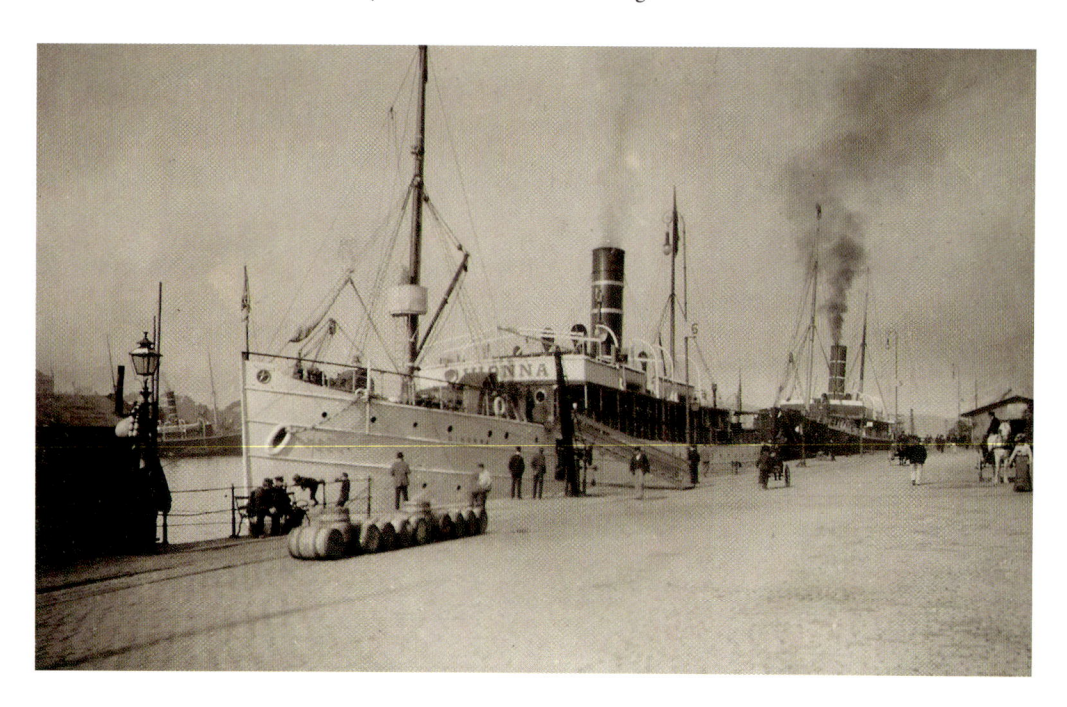

"Oihonna" moored in Bergen, 1902.

Russian sailing fleet in Hammerfest, 1902.

Captain Bade (dark cap on left) and crew amongst Lapps and reindeer herd, Lyngseidet, 1902.

A successful hunting party, "Oihonna", 1902.

The timetable for the 1906 cruises, as presented in Bade's tourist brochure:

Outward Journey

First cruise	Second cruise	Itinerary
4th July	4th August	Evening boarding in Kiel
5th July	5th August	Departure early morning from Kiel
5th July	5th August	Cruise amongst Danish Islands
6th July	6th August	Passage from Skagen to Lindesnes
7th July	7th August	Start of cruise amongst Norwegian islands
8th July	8th August	Cruise in Geirangerfjord with landing at Merok (7hr stay)
9/10th July	9/10th August	Torghatten and Arctic Circle
10th July	10th July	Arrive Lofoten Islands and land at Raftsund (3hr stay)
11th July	11th August	Arrive Tromsø, Post Office (approx 12 hrs)
12th July	12th August	Landing at Hammerfest, Post office (approx 4 hrs).
12th July	12th August	Landing at Nordkapp (approx 4 hrs).
13th July	13th August	Passage to Bjørnøya
14th July	14th August	Arrive Spitsbergen

Time in Spitsbergen

Remain in area for approximately 5 days

The places to be visited can only be determined on the spot and depend on the weather conditions. If interested consider booking from the following:
- Isfjorden and Sassenbukta (opportunities for private hunting trips).
- Virgohamna and Andrée's balloon station.
- Smeerenburg with its graves and whaling remains from the seventeenth century.
- Bellsund and Recherchefjorden (whaling station).
- Magdalenefjorden with Adambreen.

If time and weather conditions permit other sites may be visited. The final aim is to reach a latitude of 80°N. At least the midnight sun will be seen.

"Oihonna's" passengers visit Grønfjorden, 1902.

"Oihonna's" crew and band.

"Oihonna's" party, 1902.

The first French tourists to visit Spitsbergen, 1902.

93

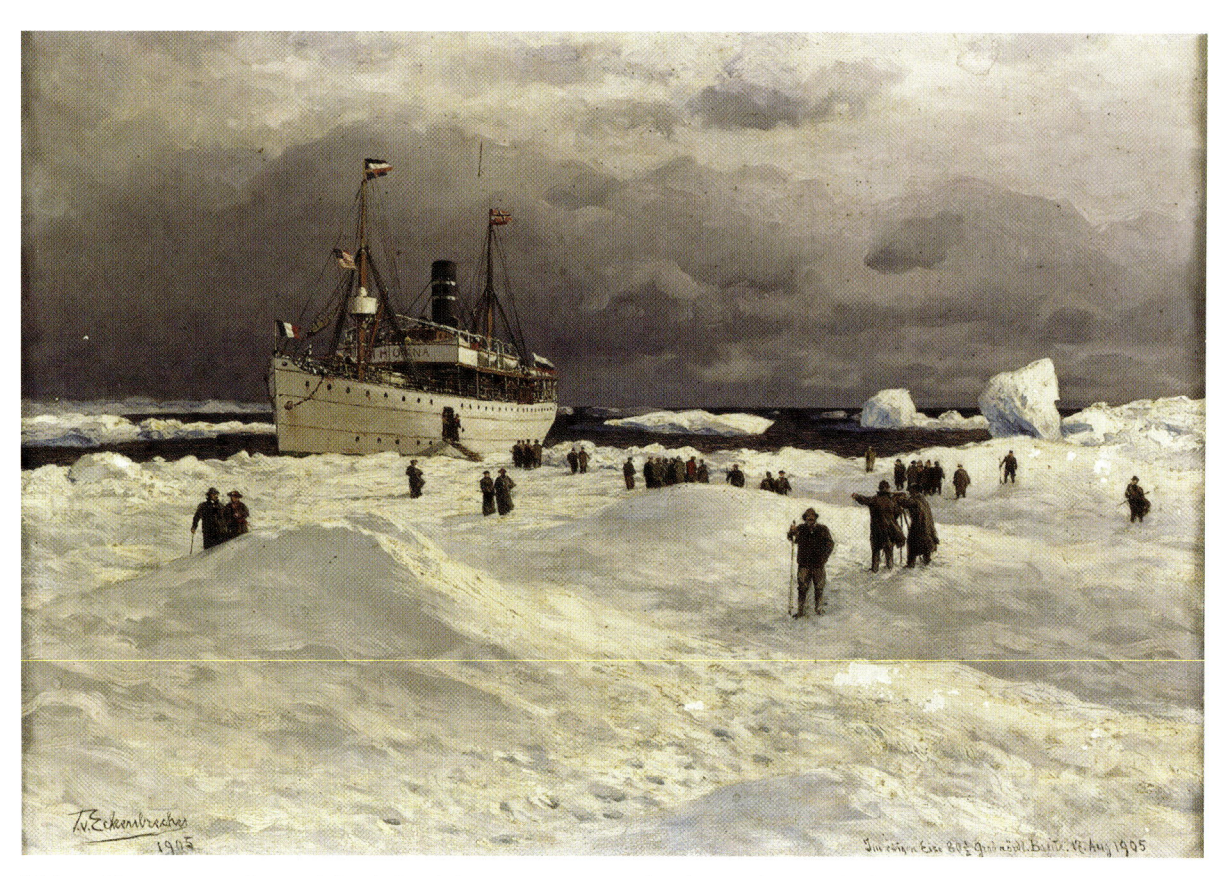

"Oihonna's" tourists on pack-ice at 80° 30' N, 17th August, 1905. Painting by Themistocles von Eckenbrecher.

...nday service onboard "Oihonna", Spitsbergen, 1902.

"Oihonna" at 80°15' N, 1902.

Return Journey

ca. 18th July	18th August	Start of return cruise
20th July	20th August	Landing at Hammerfest, Post office (approx 5 hrs)
21st July	21st August	Landing at Lyngenfjord. Visit to cloths store (approx 4 hrs)
21st July	21st August	Landing at Tromsø. Post Office (approx 8 hrs).
22nd July	22nd August	Passage to Bodø
22/23rd July	22/23rd August	Passage to Arctic Circle
23rd July	23rd August	Landing at Torgen Island (ascent of Torghatten, approx 2 hrs)
24th Jluy	24th August	Landing at Drontheim. Post Office (approx 14 hrs)
25th July	25th August	Romsdalfjord and landing at Andalsnaes (approx 6 hrs).
25/26th July	25/26th August	Landing at Molde, Post office, (approx 18 hrs).
26th July	26th August	Passage to Ålesund
27th July	27th August	Sognefjord, Naerofjord with Landing at Gudvangen. Post Office (approx 7 hrs).
		Excursion to Stalheim. Departure point for overland tour Vossevangen – Bergen.
28/29th July	28/29th August	Landing at Bergen. Post Office (approx 24 hrs).
29th July	29th August	Passage to Kopervik
30th July	30th August	Passage to Skagen
31st July	31st August	Arrive in Kiel

These cruises were very popular and were deemed worthy of mention in the respected Baedeker's guide books. The following entry, for example, appeared in the *Norway and Sweden* edition of 1903: *"From Hammerfest to Spitzbergen. About 750 kil (465 Engl M.). The steamer takes about 2½ days, but there is now no regular service since the Vesteraalens Dampskibs-Selskab discontinued the service. The best way to get a glimpse of the polar regions is to join one of the pleasure-cruises arranged by Capt. Bade (Wismar, Mecklenburg, Germany) who makes two voyages (in July and August) of four weeks in duration, skirting the Norwegian coast and going to Spitzbergen (where a stay of 4-5 days is made). The food and appointments on board his vessel are well spoken of; inclusive fares, berth £40-75, stateroom for one person £90."*

Hunting trips were a regular feature of these early cruises and their activity, not surprisingly, led to a drastic reduction in the reindeer population. Leclerc, a tourist on the 1902 cruise, wrote an emotional appeal for the slaughter to cease after witnessing the results of a hunting party: *"They have killed ten, of which seven have been carried aboard by our crew. Oh! The cruel sport! I felt pity especially for a young fawn full of grace and kindness, now lifeless. The poor thing has still in its mouth a tuft of moss which it was grazing at the moment of its death. Isn't it revolting! If the hunters, a breed without compassion and with scientific indifference, continue to depopulate Spitsbergen, the last retreat of the wild deer, this living relic of the Ice-Age will become extinct … Is it necessary for them to massacre without reason, for the sole pleasure of killing?"*

This seasonal activity continued unabated and by 1914 the population had reached a nadir of round 1,000 individuals. Recently, Carpine-Lancre and Barr have documented the warnings given by Albert I of Monaco in 1913: *"The local animals are stupidly massacred by certain tourists whom cruise ships or yachts bring north. These unscrupulous and short-sighted people derive a stupid pleasure from shooting hundreds of inedible birds, reindeer whose carcasses are left lying, and seals whose bodies sink to the sea-bed. The sight of such behaviour is repugnant to any sensible person. It is all the more irritating, in that these animals have a natural trust that allows the intelligent tourist to wonder among them, as if among animals in an ornamental park. The creation of reserves would certainly be very effective."*

Such concerns eventually led Norway to implement regulatory measures to protect the environment. Reindeer were seen as a priority and hunting was banned as early as 1925, a measure that saved them from extinction. Today, this unique species (*Rangifer tarandus platyrhynchis*) has recovered to around 12,000 animals, located mainly in central Spitsbergen, Edgeøya, Barentsøya and Nordaustlandet.

A number of "Oihonna's" passengers deserve mention. Arthur Berson and Hermann Elias, both Austrian meteorologists and aeronauts, joined the 1902 cruise. Berson had achieved international fame for breaking the world altitude record for a manned balloon flight. On 31 July 1901, together with Reinard Süring, he had ascended to a height of 10,820 metres in the "Preussen", a record that stood until 1931. Both balloonists, however, collapsed on the descent, before fortunately regaining consciousness at around 7,000 metres. His enthusiasm for ballooning remained undiminished and he employed them to make many important meteorological observations Indeed, Berson continued his research during "Oihonna's" Spitsbergen cruise and together with Elias proved the feasibility of flying kites from ships at sea. Despite the tight schedule, Bade agreed to alter "Oihonna's" speed and course to ensure that the experiments were carried out safely. With borrowed equipment from the Tegel Observatory, including kite, hoist and wire, the two men accomplished twenty-eight ascents, reaching a height of a kilometre and, in doing so, obtained the first high atmospheric measurements anywhere in the polar region.

Albert Brun, a Swiss volcanologist, used the 1902 cruise to make a brief exploration of the southern coast of Sassenfjorden. In the company of four other passengers, Brun ascended Flower Valley (Flowerdalen) to reach the summit of an unclimbed 917-metre peak (now known as Albert Bruntoppen), lying due west of Lusitaniafjellet. A small cairn was built on the summit, in which they placed a bottle containing their maps, details of the route taken and copies of their geological and meteorological observations.

The Greek-German landscape and naval painter, Karl Paul Themistocles von Eckenbrecher, was one of fifty-one passengers on the second 1905 cruise. Like many before him, Eckenbrecher was captivated by the atmospheric clarity of the high arctic and the grandeur of Spitsbergen's scenery. He undertook many sketches during the cruise, some of which were subsequently used to illustrate postcards, while others were used as studies for more formal works.

Whalers in Bellsund (Themistocles von Eckenbrecher, 1905).

Glacial snout in Bellsund (Themistocles von Eckenbrecher, 1905).

99

Finally, Aemilius Hacker, an Austrian mountaineer and ski pioneer, used the 1905 schedule to undertake a four-man mountaineering expedition to central Spitsbergen. The original plan was to establish camp in Wijdefjorden, but Bade, not surprisingly, feared that the ice conditions would be too unpredictable to guarantee a safe passage. Hacker eventually settled on Dickson Land and arranged to sail with two companions in July, spend a month exploring the mountains either side of Billefjorden, and be picked up by the "Oihonna" on her return voyage. In Tromsø, additional rations and equipment were purchased, as well as Admiralty maps, while in Hammerfest a Norwegian hunter and his dog joined the team. During the four weeks ashore, the climbers explored a wide area and made a number of first ascents although, unfortunately, their charts were not sufficiently accurate to enable their claims to be accepted. It is for this reason that geographical names, such as Klaas-Billen-Peak, Johannispass and Johannisberg, do not appear on today's maps. When ready to depart, the four adventurers believed that they had been abandoned, since the "Oihonna" failed to rendezvous on the agreed date. Their favoured explanation was that war had broken out between Sweden and Norway and that the cruise had been cancelled. The truth, however, was more prosaic – the continual daylight and frequent spells of fog had caused the climbers to loose twenty-four hours and resulted in their arrival a day early!

Midnight on Klaus-Billen-Peak, with Billefjorden (centre) and Isfjorden (far right). Hacker, 1905.

Thalia

In 1907, Axel Bade chartered the 2,896-ton "Thalia" from the Österreichischen Lloyds (Austrian Lloyd) based in Trieste, which at the time was part of Austria. She was built in Scotland in 1886 and after an extensive refit in 1907 was able to carry 171 first class passengers. The first cruise was from Bremerhaven to Trondheim in July, but two days after her return she embarked on a more extensive cruise to Spitsbergen, with visits to Isfjorden, Sassenfjorden (with opportunities for reindeer hunting), Virgohamna (Andrée's and Wellman's base camps), Smeerenburgfjorden and the pack-ice. Prices ranged from 800 Marks for a single cabin to 2500 Marks for luxury *en-suite* facilities.

Österreichischen Lloyds subsequently organised their own Spitsbergen cruises in the "Thalia" in 1908 and 1909, making two trips on each occasion, and again with single trips in 1910 and 1913. The 1908 cruise, however, was notable for its encounter with Theodore Lerner, the eccentric German adventurer who figures prominently in the island's history. Having wintered in Adventfjorden, he sledged across to Virgohamna and then over the mountains to Raudfjorden.

After completing one of the most impressive and least known sledge trips in Svalbard's history, Lerner spent the summer months surveying parts of the north coast. Finally, he sought a passage home on the "Thalia" and whilst onboard met Lydia Stoltze, a Frankfurter beauty. The two immediately fell in love and became engaged, whilst in the pack-ice at 80° N.

"Thalia" after her conversion to a saloon ship in 1907.

A brochure for "Thalia's" 1908 cruise to Spitsbergen, led by Axel Bade.

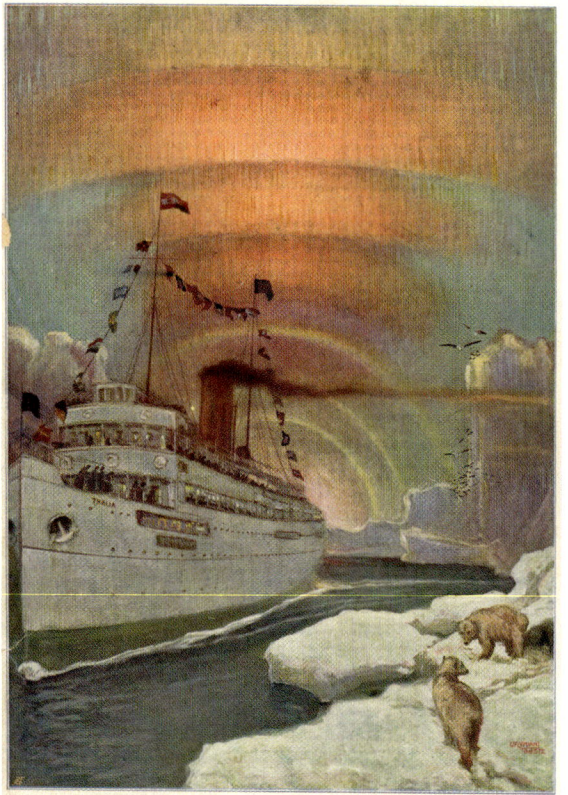

Österreichischen Lloyds activities were suspended at the outbreak of war and were not re-established until 1919, under the Italian flag as Lloyd Triestino, although cruises to Spitsbergen were never reinstated.

Andenæs

The last cruise organised by the Bade family was in 1908, when the "Andenæs", a relatively new 813-ton steamship built by A/S Fredriksstad Mek. Verksted, was chartered from the Vesteraaalens Dampskipsselskap (VDS). She departed from Kiel for the 28-day voyage to Spitsbergen, although her next polar cruise was not until 1911, when the VDS organised its own tours for a further three consecutive seasons.

Norwegian Cruises

Vesteraalens Dampskibssewlskap

In 1891, August Gran, the national steam ship advisor, proposed the establishment of an express shipping service between Trondheim and Hammerfest and convinced the government to set aside 150,000 crowns for the project. Two steamship companies, Nordenfjeldske Dampskibsselskap (NDS - Northern Steamship Company) and Bergenske Dampskibsselskab (BDS - Bergen Steamship Company), were offered the route, but declined believing that travel during the dark and stormy winters was impossible. At the time, there were only two marine charts in existence and only 28 lighthouses north of Trondheim.

In contrast, the Vesteraalens Dampskibsselskap (VDS - Vesteraalens Steamship Company), a relatively young company based in Stokmarknes took up the challenge. The entrepreneurial manager, Richard With, who had established the company in 1881 with profits from the Lofoten herring fishery, convinced the authorities of the feasibility of his plan. On 18th May 1893, the government signed a 4-year contract

Richard Bernhard With (1846–1930) established a weekly summer cruise to Spitsbergen in 1896.

with VDS and provided financial backing for a weekly sailing between Trondheim and Hammerfest in the summer and Trondheim and Tromsø during the winter. When the steamship "Vesterålen" left the quay at Trondheim it signalled the beginning of a communication revolution for the peoples of northern Norway. This first Hurtigrute, or "Sportsman's Route", along Norway's arctic coastline was a great success, with the service continuing to the present day. Indeed, its profitability encouraged the VDS to expand and in 1896 it introduced regular summer cruises from Tromsø to Spitsbergen, in the 350-ton "Lofoten".

Schedule for "Lofoten's" six cruises to Spitsbergen, 1896 (Årbok Svalbard).

Lofoten

The "Lofoten" sailed from Hammerfest some two hours after the arrival of the Hurtigrute's "Vesterålen" and the popularity of these cruises led the company to operate a weekly service throughout July and August for the next three summers. In 1897, for example, she made seven trips to Spitsbergen, each lasting six days, with Otto Sverdrup as captain. The forty-two year old skipper was well suited to the post, having been to sea from the age of seventeen. In 1888 he had accompanied Nansen on the first crossing of Greenland and later achieved fame for skippering the "Fram" on her momentous arctic voyages.

The ambitious plans of the VDS extended to the building of a hotel at Adventfjorden enabling tourists, lured by "opportunities for hunting and fishing in the Arctic" to remain ashore for several days. The return fare was

Otto Sverdrup (1854–1930), captain of the "Lofoten"

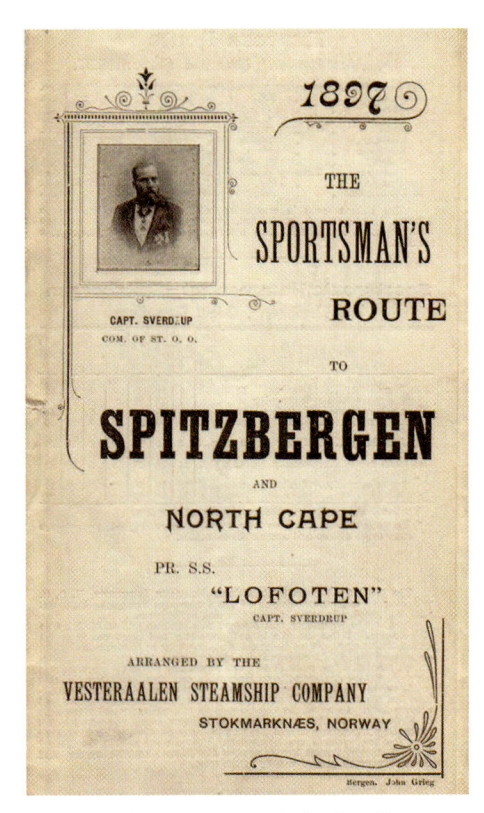

A VDS brochure advertising the "Lofoten's" 1897 cruise to Spitsbergen (courtesy of the National Archives of Norway).

The hotel was constructed from numbered wooden boards and posts supplied by M. Thams & Co., Løkken.

360 kroner and included one week's board at the hotel. The later was constructed from numbered wooden boards and posts that had been transported by the "Raftsund", the same vessel that carried Sir Martin Conway's expedition and the Swedish journalist, Stadling, who had planned to cover

105

A faience plate depicting the tourist hotel, produced by Villeroy & Boch, Mettlach, Germany, in 1898 as a souvenir (courtesy of Siegfried Nichlas).

Andrée's North Pole expedition for his newspaper, *Aftonbladet*. All available hands were employed in rafting the building material ashore, in what turned out to be a race against the encroaching pack-ice. Within a week the hotel was finished with the exception of the roof, which consisted of birch bark over wooden battens and tarred felt. According to Studley, the roof was, *"finally covered with semi-green sods cut from the fast-thawing out banks in the immediate vicinity"*.

The hotel, a sort of alpine hut, offered sleeping accommodation and simple meals for up to twenty-five visitors. Bedrooms

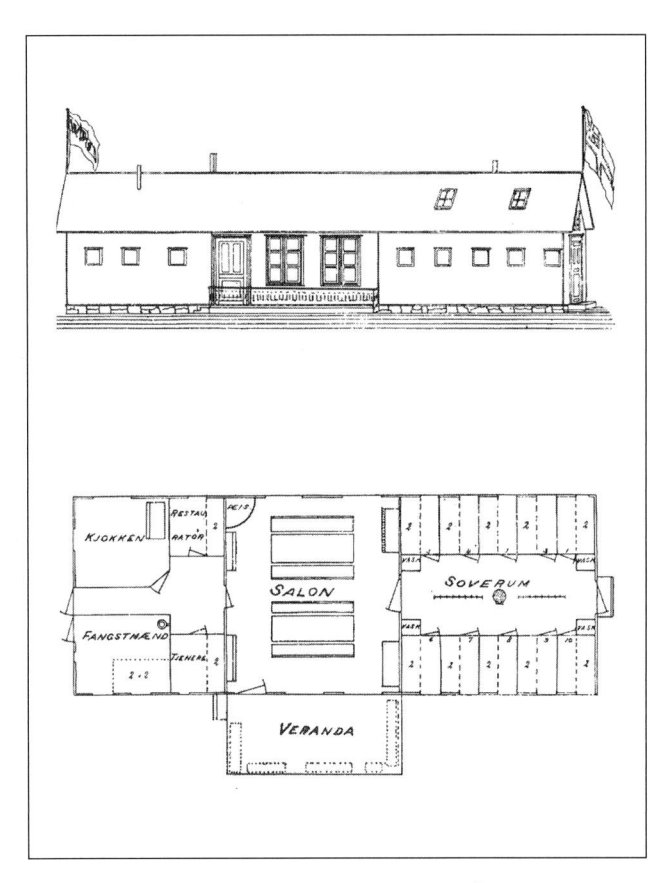

An early plan for the tourist hotel at Adventfjorden (Årbok Svalbard).

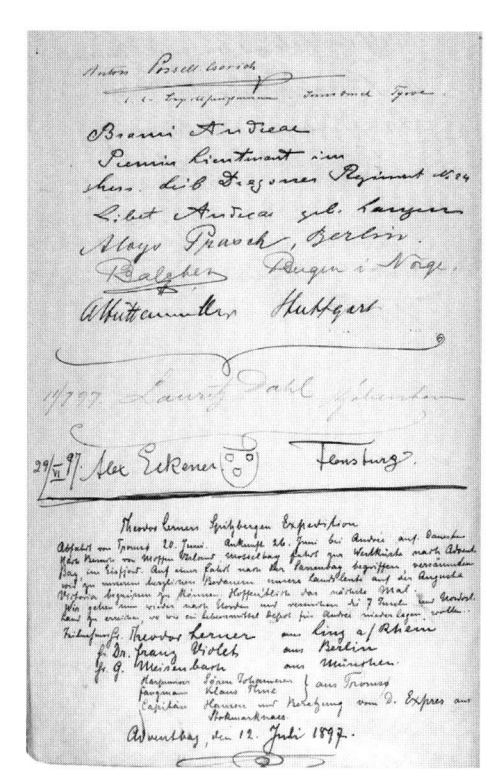

The Hotel guest book, June–July 1897. Note signatures of the German three-man tourist expedition (Theodor Lerner, Franz Violet and G. Meisenbach), who had just returned from Andrée's base camp in the "Express". Alex Eckener, a German painter and lithographer, visited the hotel on 29th July (courtesy of the National Archived of Norway).

The Spitsbergen Gazette, "the most northern newspaper in the world" (Hoel, 1966–67).

were furnished with a single bunk-bed and opened onto a central corridor that housed a cast-iron, stove. A large communal room, furnished with two large trestle tables and a piano provided the focal point for the guests. Emil Ellingsen, the manager, also acted as sub-postmaster and sold the first Spitsbergen stamps to tourists, as well as the Spitsbergen Gazette, "the most northern newspaper on the globe". The paper, issued weekly during July and August, was edited by the schoolmaster Carl Christensen in Tromsø, were it was probably also printed. The annual subscription for residents in Norway, Sweden and Denmark was 5 kroner, while for those in England six shillings and in Germany six marks. The hotel was not a success, however, and was only used for two seasons. It remained empty until 1908, when it was purchased by the Arctic Coal Company and moved to Longyear City. This iconic and much photographed building ended up as the mining community's shop and storehouse until it was finally destroyed by the Germans in 1943.

The "Lofoten" also provided transport for several hunting parties and their equipment. The five-man party of Johan Hagerup, for example, was put ashore at Midterhuken, in Bellsund, together with stores that included three rowing

A wrapper for the Spitsbergen Gazette that was mailed to Christiania in 1897 and carried by the "Lofoten". The paper's nine issues were published July-August 1897 and contained articles relating to Spitsbergen, in German, Norwegian and English. The gazette was sold to visiting tourists, although a few were posted to subscribers in Europe in its special wrapper.

boats and building material for several huts. The most unusual group, however, consisted of seven individuals, from two families, who planned to spend the winter of 1898-99 in the company's hotel at Adventfjorden. The party, which included two women and a three year-old child, established a temporary base, while waiting for the hotel to be vacated, and in doing so provided a focus of curiosity for visiting tourists. Indeed, those on board the "Auguste Victoria" took a particular interest in their plans and urged the party's leader to hoist a flag to indicate that all was well when they returned next year. Before departing, the Germans wished them luck and sang *Sønner av Norge, det eldgamle rike* (*Children of Norway, the ancient kingdom*), to the sounds of the ship's orchestra. The overwinterers fared well at first, with good hunting that produced a total of 7 polar bears, 70 foxes, 40 reindeer and 100 kilograms of down. However, the hotel's thin walls and lack of insulation forced them to use their warmer tents for accommodation. In addition, the first signs of scurvy manifested in the spring and by early summer several individuals were severely debilitated. The sickest member sought urgent help and returned home onboard the "Auguste Victoria" in mid-July, while the rest waited for their scheduled return in the "Lofoten".

The VDS also kept a small vessel in Spitsbergen, the twelve-ton "Express", to enable tourists to sightsee up and down the coast. A number took the opportunity of calling in on Andrée's base camp on Danskøya, while others undertook hunting excursions in and around Isfjorden. The German journalist, Theodor Lerner, for example, hired the vessel to take his party to meet Andrée and in the end provided valuable assistance by laying a small depot of provisions and ammunition on Sjuøyane. Also on board was Alexander Eckener, a painter and lithographer, who made many drawings of his trip, some of which were used to illustrate the *Spitzbergen Gazette*. On other occasions, the "Express" brought eagerly awaited mail for Andrée's team, while its most ambitious trip was to take Sir Martin Conway's expedition on a flying visit along Spitsbergen's northern coast, including a foray down Hinlopenstretet. Later, two of Conway's expedition members hired the vessel in an attempt to climb the 1,431-metre Hornsundtind, an impressive mountain that dominates the southern shore of Hornsund. They failed and the two adventurers were forced to return to mainland Europe onboard the "Express", having missed their rendezvous with the "Lofoten". The small number of tourists taking part in these cruises often produced a spirit of camaraderie and a resultant party-like atmosphere. This can be deduced from the reminiscences of a Norwegian tourist from 1896, recorded in the Spitsbergen Gazette:

Our doctor was a lively fellow, and true to his calling, he, of course, felt obliged to doctor us, but his usual prescription was so good that I will repeat it for the benefit of others. The dose is:

1 cup strong coffee,
sugar and condensed milk,
mixed with a quantum satis of Martell & Co.

This is an excellent drink on a cold evening, and many were the doses we took, singing, at the same time, Norwegian or English songs; Mr Holland recited a grand épos, which he had composed, about the storm in Hinlopen Strait and the wonderful shooting exploit on Cloven Cliff; the Eton and Christiania students treated us to some of their special numbers also. Dr Holmboe's doses (Norwegian coffee-doctors they were unanimously dubbed) doubtless had the effect of making our English friends invite us, and the whole company at Advent Bay, on our arrival there to an English evening. After a splendid supper, Mr Barneby and Mr Walkey disappeared into the pantry, coming back shortly afterwards with a tureenful of "champagne-punch". The ingredients were champagne, curaçao, soda-water, cinnamon, cloves and many other species; it was served in champagne glasses, and I thought it was excellent.

There were representatives of our nations present. In addition to our English hosts, there were two English ladies, Miss Harvey and Miss Hearn; Baron de Geer and Lieutenant von Knorring represented Sweden. From Germany were Dr Hänsel and Hr. Rehnert; and then there were we three Norwegians. After supper, the ladies had withdrawn to go to their tiny bedrooms, but a deputation was sent to wait upon them, and ask them "to smoke their cigars with the gentlemen, "whereupon they laughingly came back, and by their presence added much pleasure to our evening. Several speeches, all in English, were made in succession.

The "Express" was again busy the following year, ferrying tourists around the island, including visits to observe Andree's second and final attempt on the Pole. Lerner, together with two fellow tourists, Meiserbach and Violet, were the first to arrive, having suffered a particularly bad crossing from Tromsø in the "Express". After handing over mail to Andrée's team, the three headed north to Mosselbutka, before returning to Virgohamna to welcome "Lofoten's" arrival.

Three German tourists, Theodore Lerner (left), G. Meisenbach (fourth from left), Dr Violet (third from right) pose with members of Andrée's expedition, 9th July 1897 (courtesy of the Grenna Museum).

111

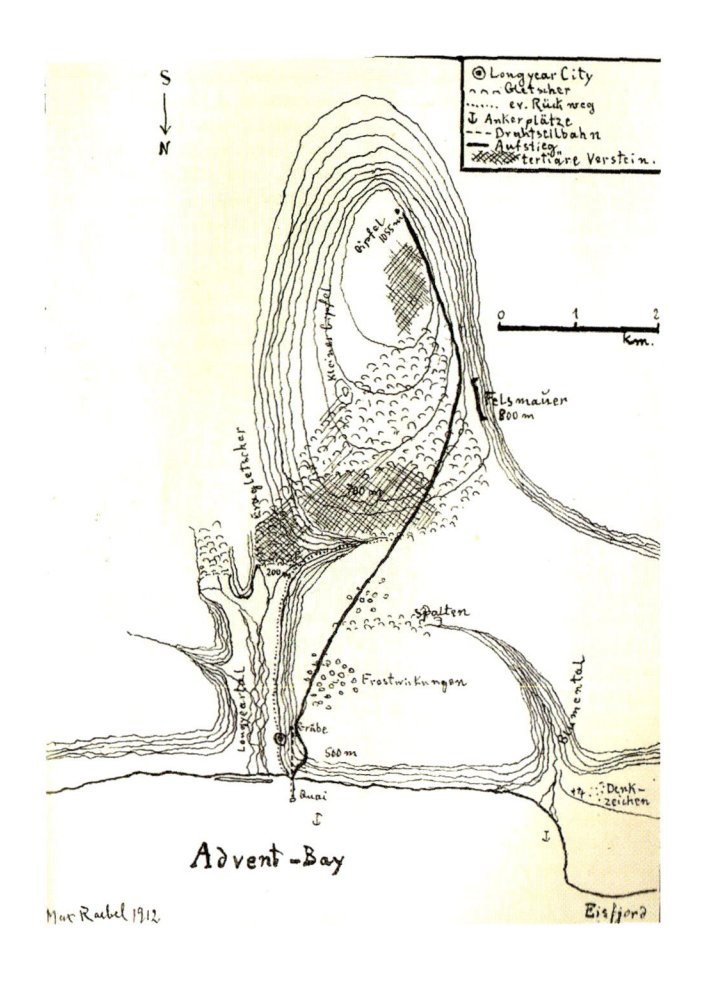

German tourist route-map showing the ascent of Nordenskiöldfjellet (1912).

Lerner's party delayed for several weeks to witness Andrée's departure, while the "Lofoten" kept to her busy schedule, plying between the mainland and Adventfjorden.

Later that summer, the "Express" was involved in a venture that nearly led to disaster. The VDS's manager, Richard With, had agreed to help a four-man English expedition reach its base camp at Kapp Thordsen, on the north side of Isfjorden. The men were left with the promise of being collected later in the season, but unfortunately, With returned to Europe without informing the "Express's" crew of the arrangements. By chance, the abandoned men were rescued by a Norwegian whaler, after it made an unscheduled visit to find water.

A popular excursion, for those based at the hotel, was the ascent of the 1,050-metre Nordenskiöldfjellet, with its wonderful panoramic views. The direct route is steep and tiring and involves crossing the barren summit plateau of Platåberget, with its extensive polygonal soils and scree, as well as boggy areas formed as a result of the underlying

Gustav Nordenskiöld in 1890. The area is rich in plant fossils, dating from the 50 million year-old Tertiary period, with species that are very similar to those found growing in lower latitudes today. The large moraines at the head of Longyeardalen, which originate from the fossil-bearing strata, provided tourists with a wealth of souvenirs.

The VDS ceased to offer tours to Spitsbergen after the 1898 season, thereby allowing the route to be dominated by German and British cruise ships. Indeed, it was not until 1911 that the company recommenced its activities, when the 817-ton "Andenæs" made its first of three voyages.

Nordenfjeldske (NDS) & Bergenske Dampskibsselskap (BDS)

After the VDS withdrew from the Spitsbergen route, Norwegian companies were surprisingly slow to fill the gap. It was not until 1906 that NDS and BDS joined forces to offer summer cruises to the island. Vessels from both com-

View of Longyearbyen and Adventfjorden in foreground, with Platåberget and Nordenskiöldfjellet behind (Norsk Polarintitutt).

permafrost. Those that reached the summit would have found a three-foot cairn, built by the Swedish explorer,

Route map from 1906 BDS/NDS brochure.

The great hole of Torghatten (courtesy Norsk Folkemuseum).

panies sailed on the same schedule, as a matter of safety, and accompanied each other throughout the entire twenty-six day voyage. The "Neptun" (BDS) departed from Antwerp, while the "Kong Harald" (NDS) set sail from Hamburg. British passengers travelled from Newcastle on the "Vega" and transferred to their allotted ship in Bergen, an arrangement that continued for six years. However, during the summers 1912 to 1914, the "Vega" replaced the "Neptun" on the Spitsbergen route.

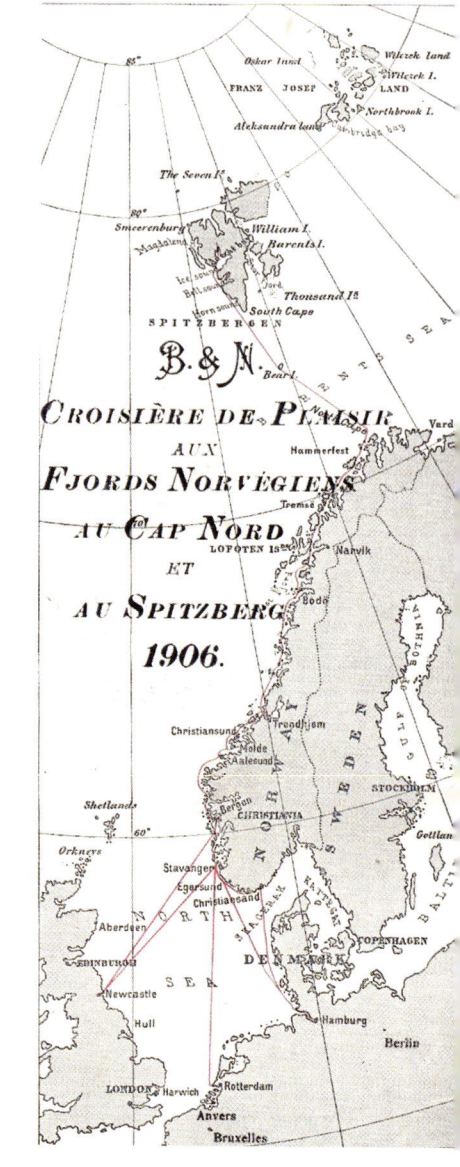

The two ships cruised northwards, half a mile apart, along the Inner Lead, the waterway that lies between the mainland and the fringe of islands that form an almost unbroken line along the entire coast of Norway. At the Arctic Circle the two vessels would draw alongside each other and mark the precise moment with a salute of four guns and the attachment of flags from many nations to their masts. Torghatten, an island shaped like a fisherman's hat with a great hole 150 metres above sea-level, was a favourite with the tourists. The voyage then entered the beautiful Raftsund, in the Lofoten group, before proceeding via Tromsø and Hammerfest to Nordkapp. Here many tourists would make the 307-metre ascent and have their pictures taken

Day excursion in Tromsø, 1910.

115

"Kong Harald" and "Neptun" off Nordkapp, 1906.

at the northernmost point of Europe by the official ship's photographer.

Twenty-four hours later, the vessels would arrive at Bjørnøya, where shore visits were arranged if the weather conditions permitted. This was infrequent, however, as the island's position, at the junction of the warm Gulf Stream and the cold eastern air current, results in the area being almost perpetually engulfed in fog. Indeed, the ice-pilot on these cruises is reported to have seen Bjørnøya only three times in thirty-six voyages. Even when the weather allowed, landing was not without risk. Hoenshel, a passenger on the 1910 cruise, tells how the engines on his motor boat failed, resulting in the craft drifting out to sea. Luckily a signal alerted the "Kong Harald" and a rescue boat towed them ashore. Unperturbed, the more adventurous tourists then scaled the steep cliffs and obtained wonderful views across the island, including distant glimpses of the abandoned whale station at Kvalrossbukta.

Recherchefjorden was next on the itinerary and shore excursions gave passengers the opportunity to explore the slopes around Renardbreen on the fjord's western coast. Glacier walks, little auk colonies and spectacular scenery made the area a favourite attraction. Visits were also made to Giæverhuset, a summer house built in 1904 for the consul of Tromsø, Johannes Giæver, who planned to profit from the growing tourism. A post office operated from the house in 1907, although it was transferred to Grønfjorden the following year. Giæverhuset still stands today, despite the considerable distortion and

"Kong Harald" steaming into Bellsund. Renardbreen and Activekammen are on the right.

Tourists exploring the whaling settlement at Grønfjorden (courtesy Norsk Folkemuseum)

"Kong Harald" and "Neptun" anchored off the old wharf, Adventfjorden (courtesy Norsk Folkemuseum).

structural damage caused by a century of storms and permafrost.

Between 1906 and 1912, tourists had the opportunity of visiting the whaling station at Grønfjorden. The notorious waste of Spitsbergen's whalers, in that only the best blubber was processed, resulted in many decaying carcasses floating around the harbour, covering the surface with a thick coating of oil and grease. The bay would have also been festooned with thousands of sea birds, especially fulmars, feeding on the floating debris. In 1911, the Norwegian government set up a Radio Station nearby, where a post office operated during the summer months to handle the whalers' mail. Post was transported back and forth by a regular boat service from Tromsø, with the "Kong Harald" and the VDS's steamer "Andenæs" providing assistance in 1913.

The next shore excursion would have been a brief tour of Longyear City, which at that time consisted of no more than

"Kong Harald's" tourists visit Adventfjorden (courtesy Norsk Folkemuseum).

Klaus Thue (left) selling souvenirs to visiting tourist ships (courtesy Norsk Folkemuseum).

a dozen houses and a few shops and outbuildings. Tourists could walk from the wharf, which was used to load colliers and which was connected to Mine 1 by a ropeway, to the head of Longyeardalen. Those fit enough to scramble up the five hundred feet to the mine entrance were offered a rather uncomfortable, candle-lit tour of the low horizontal galleries that penetrated the hillside. Later, the two Norwegian ships, having taken on board coal, would proceed, via Hotellneset and Advent City, to Sassenfjorden for a five-hour stay. This wide, relatively fertile valley, offered good sport for the hunting parties, while others could take the opportunity to hike inland, collect fossils or study the arctic flora.

The cruises then ventured north, offering dramatic views of Krossfjorden, Lilliehöökfjorden, Möllerfjorden, as well as Danskøya and

The main street, Longyear City (post-1910). The building on the left is the hotel purchased by the Arctic Coal Company in 1908.

Coal miners at Longyear City pose for the tourist camera.

Amsterdamøya. The shallow draft of the Norwegian ships enabled them to navigate deep into the fjords, allowing close encounters with the vertical ice walls of the glacier snouts. Another highlight of these tours was a visit to Virgohamna, where visitors could meet the American explorer, Walter Wellman. Tours were arranged of his extensive base camp, complete with its large airship hangar, living quarters, machine shop, hydrogen gas apparatus, boiler and pumping houses and two hundred tons of gas making material. Wellman, who was financed by the *Chicago Record-Herald*, was attempting to become the first person to reach the North Pole. His own account of the expedition gives few details of the encounters with tourist ships, but fortunately a Norwegian newspaper (*Tromsøposten*, 28 August 1906) printed a telegram detailing the events:

Mine 1, also called the "American Mine", from Longyear City. Note the hillside hoist linking the town (left) and the first ropeway, in which coal was carried in telphers, or carriers, travelling in a system of overhead traction supported by large wooden trestles (right).

"Neptun" in Lilliehöökfjorden (courtesy Norsk Folkemuseum).

"Kong Harald's" passengers pose for the camera in Wellman's balloon hangar (courtesy Norsk Folkemuseum).

Wellman and the other participants of the expedition gave us a charming reception. We were afforded the opportunity to inspect everything. The colossal balloon-shed, whose skeleton is nearly full erected, as well as machines and equipment, the site and remains of Andrée's balloon shed, Mr Pike's house.... Wellman and Major Hersey, the expedition's American participants, were invited to dinner onboard the Kong Harald. Some especially interested passengers from the Neptun were also invited. Passengers immediately seized glasses, cups and spoons used by Wellman while he was onboard and then demanded certificates authenticating there spoils. After dinner, Wellman visited the Neptun. The passengers of both ships gave large ovations upon his de-embarkation. The general impression from conversation with Wellman was that an ascent this year, while not out of the question, all the same was considered unlikely, due to delays in the work caused by inclement weather conditions. It is most likely that the expedition

Wellman about to board the "Kong Harald" and meet the tourists.

will leave towards the end of September, leaving behind them a number of engineers and workers to take care of everything until next summer. Photographers and amateurs from the ranks of the passengers of both vessels take a large amount of photographs. Favourable group photographs were taken of the passengers of both ships as well as Andrée's stone with all nations' flags.

The climax of all these cruises – indeed it was advertised as such – was the run to the edge of the pack-ice. The crew, with the assistance of the ice-pilots, manoeuvred their vessels through the complex leads between the ice-floes, until progress was blocked. At this point, the flags of all nations represented on board were hoisted up the masts, and a salute of eight guns was given to the Polar World. A latitude of over 80 degrees was achieved most years, with 1906 being the record when the "Kong Harald" and "Neptun" reached 81° 11"N.

The pioneer photographer, Anders Beer Wilse (1865–1949), used the opportunity provided by these cruises to visit Spitsbergen many times. His *oeuvre* provides an important historical record of the island during the early part of the twentieth century and includes a valuable series of pictures of the mining settlement at Advent City before its abandonment in 1908. He also documented the activities of Wellman's North Pole Expedition and the short-lived whale fishery, as well as recording the day to day progress of the "Kong Harald" and "Neptun" in Spitsbergen waters.

Joining Wilse on the 1908 cruise was the Norwegian author, Øvre Richter Frich (1872–1945), and his editor, A. Schibsted. Wilse wrote of their time ashore, including their struggles over moraines and permafrost to observe a glacier at close quarters and their visit to an abandoned trapper's hut. The latter was noted to be a crude wooden structure made from shipped planks, augmented by driftwood, in which the architectural emphasis was on functionality rather than aesthetics. In the vicinity, they encountered the blood stained remains of the hunter's trade - fox, polar bear and reindeer skins, as well as carcasses of sea birds. A note left on the table indicated that the owner had left some weeks before, probably to return to the mainland to sell his quarry and to restock in preparation for the next season.

Hunters would travel north during late summer, or early autumn, to prepare for the harsh winter with its ever present dangers, but with significant rewards for the skilful. Indeed, the prized blue fox pelt could realise as much as 800 to 1000 kroner, while polar bears skins fetched approximately 250 kroner. The most successful hunter, Henry Rudi, was nicknamed the "polar bear king" on account of his tally of 713 bears during his forty year career in the arctic. Around one hundred men over-wintered during the ten years between 1895 and 1905, a fact likely to reflect the travel opportunities provided by the increasing number of tourist ships and mining supply vessels that were visiting the island. Merchants, such as Finckenhagen from Hammerfest and Claus Andersen, based in Tromsø, would offer to equip hunting parties in return for a percentage of the profits. Many hunters also supplemented their income by working as watchmen for the mining companies in the summer, or supplying the construction workers with fresh provisions. Karl Bengsten, for example, sold large quantities of Svalbard salmon, caught by seine nets in one of Isfjorden's bays, to an English mining company. Such activities made the difference between solvency and bankruptcy for many.

Frich was clearly fascinated by the life-style of these hardy individuals and some years later he incorporated his tourist experiences in the novel, *I Polarnattens Favn* ("In the Embrace of the Polar Night").

Captain Johannessen of the "Vega", which visited Spitsbergen in 1912 and 1913.

The "Vega" in Bellsund in 1912, by an unknown German artist.

A BDS vessel close to the snout of Lilliehöökbreen.

A BDS vessel at the edge of the pack-ice.

Tourists on board a BDS vessel in Krossfjorden.

German Cruises

Hamburg-Amerika-Linie

In 1847, venture capitalists and ship owners from Hamburg created the world famous shipping company, Hamburg-Amerika-Linie (HAPAG = Hamburg Amerikanische Packetfahrt Actien Gesellschaft) with its ambitious motto *"my field is the world"*. Not content with a substantial and lucrative emigrant business, the company explored the "cruise" concept with the "Auguste Victoria" in 1891, when she toured the Mediterranean. The resultant Teutonic enthusiasm for holiday cruises was insatiable and led the German tour companies to offer evermore adventurous destinations.

Columbia

The "Columbia", a three-masted, three funnelled steamship, built by the Laird Brothers in Birkenhead, undertook the company's inaugural arctic voyage in 1893, with subsequent visits in 1895 and 1896. The twenty day cruises departed from Hamburg, travelled along the west coast of Norway and spent some thirty-six hours in the Spitsbergen area,

Tourist brochure advertising "Columbia's" voyage to Norway and Spitsbergen, 1896.

"Columbia" off Spitsbergen's west coast.

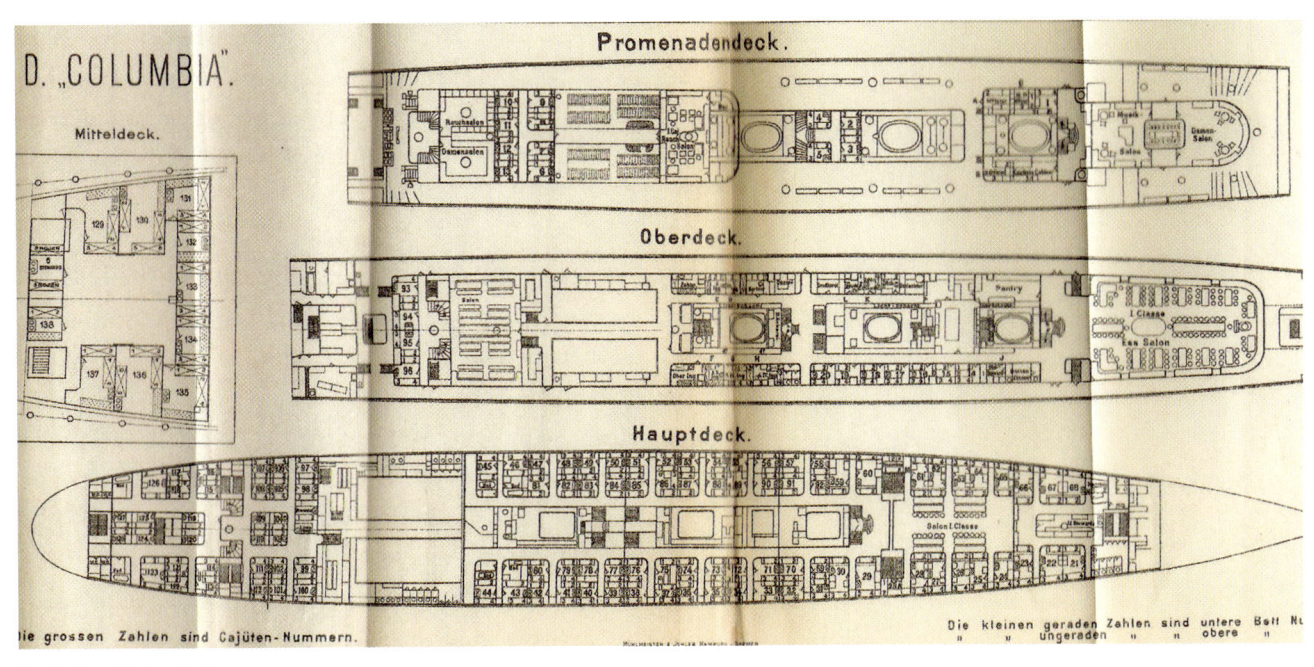

Deck plan, "Columbia".

visiting Bellsund and Isfjorden, before returning home to Cuxhaven. Prices ranged from 600 to 1,500 Marks for a twin cabin, although few daily details are known as no travelogues were written. Today, it is easy to forget the pioneering nature of these voyages, as vessels this size, 7,241 tons and 463 feet in length, had never before navigated Spitsbergen's coastal waters. Indeed, running aground on hidden reefs was a significant risk, with little chance of immediate rescue.

Fahrplan der „Columbia".

			Aufenthalt in Stunden.
15. Juli	Morgens 9 Uhr	Abfahrt von **Hamburg**.	
16. „	Nachm. 1 „	Ankunft in **Hoievarde** (Kopervik), dann Fahrt durch den **Hardanger-** und **Sörfjord**.	
16. „	Abends 9 „	Ankunft in **Odde**	22
17. „	„ 7 „	Abfahrt von **Odde**.	
18. „	Nachm. 4 „	Ankunft in **Molde**	13
19. „	Morgens 5 „	Abfahrt von **Molde**.	
19. „	„ 7 „	Ankunft in **Næs**	11
19. „	Nachm. 6 „	Abfahrt von **Næs**.	
20. „	Morgens 6 „	Ankunft in **Trondhjem**	12
20. „	Nachm. 6 „	Abfahrt von **Trondhjem**.	
22. „	„ 5 „	Ankunft am **Nordcap**	9
23. „	Vorm. 2 „	Abfahrt vom **Nordcap**.	
24. „	Abends 6 „	Ankunft in **Spitzbergen** (Icefjord) (Fahrt an der Küste, ev. Landung im **Glocken-(Bell)-Sund**.	20
25. „	Nachm. 2 „	Abfahrt von **Spitzbergen** (Icefjord).	
27. „	Morgens 6 „	Ankunft in **Tromsœ**	24
28. „	„ 6 „	Abfahrt von **Tromsœ**.	
29. „	„ 7 „	Ankunft in **Digermulen**	11
29. „	Abends 6 „	Abfahrt von **Digermulen**. (Fahrt durch den **Westfjord**, dann bei **Aalesund** in den **Nordfjord** durch den **Slyngs-** und **Sunelvfjord** in den **Geirangerfjord**	
31. „	Morgens 8 „ in Maraak	**Maraak** (Marok) und zurück auf demselben Wege, dann in den **Jörundfjord**, endlich in den **Sognefjord**, durch **Aurlands-** und **Näröfjord** bis Gudvangen.)	4
1. Aug.	Mittags 12 „	Ankunft in **Gudvangen** . . . . . (Ueberlandreisen via **Stahlheim** und **Vossevangen** nach **Bergen**.)	20
2. „	Morgens 8 „	Abfahrt von **Gudvangen**.	
2. „	Abends 6 „	Ankunft in **Bergen**	27
3. „	Abends 9 „	Abfahrt von **Bergen**.	
5. „	Morgens 5 „	Ankunft in **Cuxhaven**.	

Itinerary for "Columbia's" cruise, 1896.

"Columbia's" early voyages set two important precedents, the building of cairns, or monuments, to commemorate a ship's visit and the use of ships' cachets as postal souvenirs. Sir Martin Conway, the British alpinist and explorer, clearly thought little of cairn building and after encountering one in Adventfjorden wrote, "*… a mound of stones, bearing a board inscribed, 'S.S. Columbia', Hamburg. D. 29.7.1893' and built to commemorate a tourist drinking bout, or Kneipe*", and concluded that the "*vulgarization of Spitsbergen had begun*". Indeed, Adventpynten became a veritable cemetery of such monuments, with many being constructed from elaborate iron structures brought from Europe and fixed firmly in stone bases. Eye witnesses have described how several boatloads of bottled beer would be brought ashore, to be followed by the ship's band and finally the passengers. Patriotic toasts were freely pledged to the sound of tunes of the Fatherland. Cachets, or hand-stamps, are first recorded from "Columbia's"

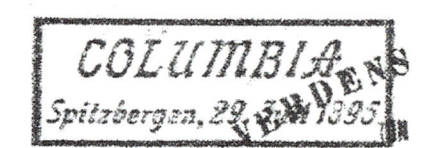

"Columbia" pioneered the use of special cachets.

voyage of 1895 and were subsequently adopted by most cruise ships. They served no official postal purpose, but did enable tourists to record their journey in the Arctic and, as a result, are highly sought after by collectors.

The "Columbia" resumed her Atlantic crossings before being sold in 1904 to the Russian Volunteer Fleet, when she was renamed "Terek" and used as a troop carrier in the Russo-Japanese War.

Auguste Victoria

The next HAPAG ship to include Spitsbergen on its itinerary was the high-speed "Auguste Victoria", which visited annually, between 1897–1903. The ship, named after Emperor Wilhelm II's wife, was launched in 1888 with a crew of 251 and with accommodation for 400 first class, 120 second class and 580 third class passengers. Her construction was at the forefront of development, in that she was one of only a few high speed steamers in the world with twin screws, as well as being the first to be built in a German shipyard, the Vulcan of Stettin. Somewhat embarrassingly, she was incorrectly named "Augusta Victoria" at launch, but was rebuilt, lengthened and renamed "Auguste Victoria" in 1897.

The ship's interior decor was luxurious in the extreme, with rococo fitments throughout, features that cost HAPAG over 200,000 Marks.

The twenty-two day cruises departed from Hamburg and spent only a few days in Spitsbergen, visiting Adventfjorden,

"Auguste Victoria's" passengers and crew, Bellsund 1897.

Nathorst's expedition ship "Antarctica" in Bellsund photographed from the "Auguste Victoria" by Dreesen in 1898.

Alfred Gabriel Nathorst (1850–1921), leader of the Swedish Spitsbergen Expedition, was invited onboard the "Auguste Victoria"

with its tourist hotel, and Bellsund, for a brief excursion to the surrounding glaciers. Unexpected encounters could add to the memorability of these cruises. For example, the German Emperor, while on his annual *Nordlandfahrt* to Norway in 1897, boarded the cruise ship and spent some time inspecting her modifications. He then invited all the tourists to join him onboard his 120 metre-long Imperial Yacht, "Hohenzollern". The Emperor loved all things Norwegian and spent a total of over four years cruising Scandinavian waters, between 1894 and 1914. In 1898, while in Recherchefjorden, the "Auguste Victoria's" captain welcomed onboard Alfred Nathorst, the Swedish explorer, whose ship "Antarctica" was anchored nearby. The Swedes had been mapping and investigating Bellsund's fjord system and had shown that the northern branch, Van Mijenfjorden, was twice as long as previously charted. Letters were exchanged before Nathorst's expedition continued north on what was to become an important circumnavigation of the archipelago and which resulted in detailed mapping of Kong Karls Land and Bjørnøya.

A number of artists and photographers joined "Auguste Victoria" as a way of increasing the sale of their works. The Hamburg photographer, Wilhelm Berges, for example, was a passenger on the 1897 and 1898 cruises. His landscapes were not only used to illustrate postcards but were also put together in lavishly bound albums, embellished with the ship's name and date, and sold to passengers as souvenirs. Frederich Kallmorgen, a German artist, sailed on the 1898 cruise, while the Swiss travel writer, Dr Elias Haffter, went in 1899. Like so many of his contemporaries, Haffter wished to share his experiences and impressions from visits to new and little-known places. His "Letters" to the local newspaper *Thurgauer Zeitung* were eventually published as a book, entitled, *Briefe aus dem hohen Norden*, and like other books by the same author, it found a wide audience and was reprinted several times.

The 1901 cruise, however, was the most significant of all, for amongst the passengers was John Munro Longyear, an American capitalist and mine owner. Longyear and his wife had undertaken the trip in response to the tragic death of their eldest son and, in so doing, set in motion a chain of events that would have a profound influence on Spitsbergen's early industrialization. The following passages

John Munro Longyear (1850–1922).

from Longyear's diary describing his first impressions cannot, therefore, fail to be of interest. Under the entry July 14, Bellsund, he wrote: *"The rock in the glacial debris seemed to be slate and slate conglomerate with much quartz. It looks to me like gold country. There was a small vessel in the Sound and our pilot told me that the men were here prospecting for coal. Spitsbergen now belongs to no country, and if coal or gold are found here some nation will hasten to colonise it."* Next day,

135

"Auguste Victoria's" tourists (1901) inspect the remains of a shelter constructed by Norwegian hunters during a forced overwintering, 1895/96.

Klaus Thue's summer camp in Adventfjorden. Each summer the Norwegian hunter sold souvenirs, including whale bones, skins and fossils, to passing tourists.

"Auguste Victoria's" passengers scramble on the lower slopes of Renardbreen, Recherchefjorden, 1898.

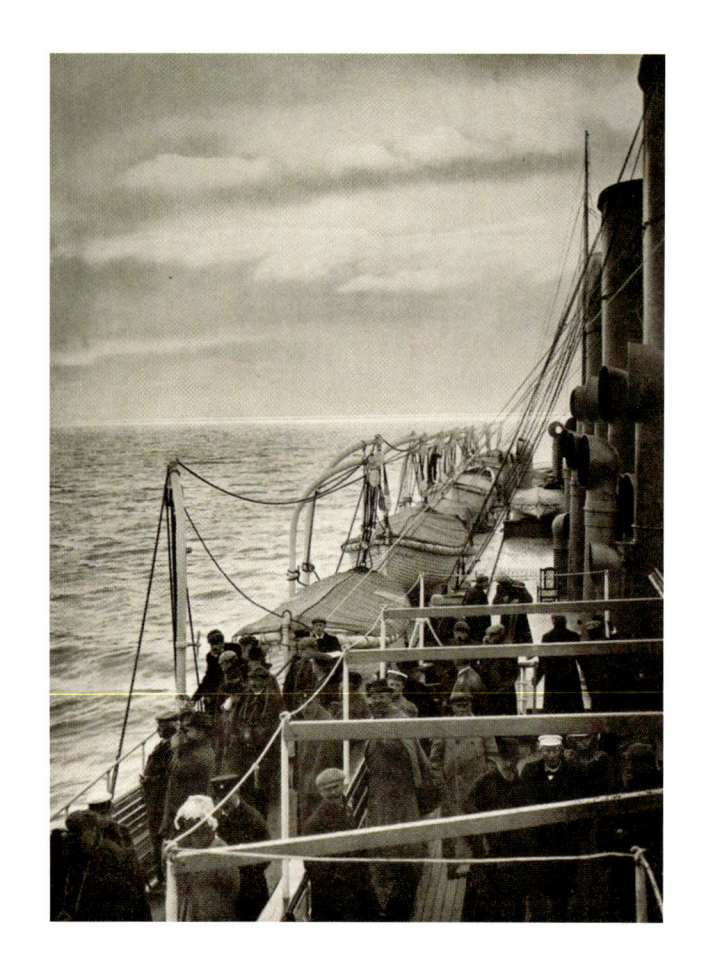

View of "Auguste Victoria's" upper deck.

"Auguste Victoria" anchored in Adventfjorden, just offshore from the tourist hotel, to give the sportsmen an opportunity to hunt. Longyear explored the shore and recorded the immediate scene: *"A little further on was the ruin of a hut in which four shipwrecked sailors and hunters spent four months. It had been made by digging a hole about ten feet square and four feet deep in the ground. Rafters had been covered with canvas, shreds of which still hung from them. An old ship's cabin door was still in place and a broken ship's window was on the ground. The old bunk of boards was still standing"*. A little further north he noted, *"On the landing place, near the hotel, were some hunters who had the only souvenirs to sell that we saw. I bought some Spitsbergen stamps which do not pay postage. They also had postcards, three polar bear skins, and other furs"*. A number of Norwegian hunters, who had spent the winter on Spitsbergen, took the opportunity of a passage home and boarded the "Auguste Victoria" with their quarry of at least fifty barrels of skins.

Longyear was clearly impressed with the commercial potential of Spitsbergen's coal deposits and he returned in 1903, again as passenger on board the "Auguste Victoria", to explore the seams in more detail. While in Recherchefjorden,

"Auguste Victoria" in Bellsund.

he went ashore with two colleagues and with a shovel borrowed from the crew, "panned" some of the gravel and sand. Not surprisingly, their primitive mining activities led some of the passengers to believe that they were prospecting for gold. The "Auguste Victoria" then sailed to Bjonahamna, a small bay on the north side of Templefjorden. Here, Longyear went ashore and took a number of photographs of the surrounding coal formations with his Kodak camera. He believed, however, that he was in Sassenfjorden, as this had been scheduled as the next stop, according to the ship's bulletin. This confusion would lead his mining syndicate, the Arctic Coal Company, to erect claim boards in the Sassenfjorden area in 1906. Back in Adventfjorden, Longyear wrote *"we saw a place where some one had dug coal out of the side of the hill, but the diggings were covered and filled with shingle which covers the hills here and everywhere except the cliffs. We went up about*

Captain Kaempff, skipper of the "Auguste Victoria", drawn by Kallmorgan, 1898.

139

"Blücher" anchored in Adventfjorden.

eight hundred feet and found more coal-diggings filled with ice, shingle etc. … He (Jeldness) reported seeing much coal in the shingle along the side of the hill west of the west outcrop and that probably the coal-seam stretched for many miles on the north side of Advent Bay – at least as far as Sassen Bay".

These thirty-six hours ashore, and the subsequent analysis of retrieved coal samples, convinced Longyear of the feasibility of coal mining in Spitsbergen and over the next few years he set about to make it a reality.

HAPAG's "dream ships"

Although the "Auguste Victoria" was a great success, the HAPAG's director, Albert Ballin, appreciated that the future cruise market called for a new type of vessel, since large steamships, taken from line service, were in general unsuitable for such activity. In 1899, Ballin ordered "a real dream ship" for his increasingly sophisticated clientele, with unprecedented standards of comfort. The German Emperor, who had a great interest in ship design, was informed of HAPAG's plans and sent his comments and suggestions, several of which were adopted. The snow-white 4,419-ton pleasure yacht, "Prinzessin Victoria Luise", named after the

Passengers await transport back to "Blücher" in Adventfjorden.

The "Blücher-Stone", built in 1904 on Adventpynten to commemorate the ship's first visit, became a focal point for shore parties and provided photographic opportunities for tourists, as on this occasion, 19th July, 1909.

Kaiser's daughter, was launched in 1900 to become the world's first ship built exclusively for cruises. She became a stunning success and visited Spitsbergen annually, between 1903–1906. Her career, however, was cut short after a freak accident when she ran aground on a sandbank outside Kingston harbour, Jamaica in 1906. The increasing size of HAPAG's ships meant more space for the designers to create the illusion that passengers were still on "terra firma". The "Prinzessin Victoria Luise" typified this transition, helped by having only 192 first class passengers and by not having to cater for cargo. Each of the 119 cabins had a living area alongside a separate bedroom and bathroom with toilet. The dining room and lounge were covered by a glass dome and she possessed a well stocked library, as well as a writing room, bar and gymnasium. There was even a state room for the Kaiser, although there is no evidence that he ever used it.

The 12,334-ton "Blücher" commenced her Spitsbergen cruises in 1904 and returned in 1906-07 and 1909–1911, while her sister ship "Moltke" visited in 1905. One of the highlights of these early cruises was a visit to the Norwegian whale fishery, located in Grønfjorden and Bellsund. Indeed, tourists on the 1904 cruise were able to witness the pioneer-

"Blücher's" dining room

The "Oceana" in Adventfjorden.

ing use of a factory ship, a technique that would achieve great success in the Southern Seas. The Norwegian vessel "Admiralen", with its two support ships, was spending its first season in the north, based in Bellsund. Tourists were ferried across in launches to observe, at close quarters, the rendering of several of the 154 whales caught that summer. Souvenirs were available, the most popular being ear bones for ten kroner a pair, fins for one kroner and canes made from skull bones.

In 1906, HAPAG replaced the "Prinzessin Victoria Luise" with the "Scot", built at Dumbarton by Denny Brothers. She was renamed "Oceana" and placed on a high-speed winter service from Naples to Alexandria, Egypt. In the summer she was used for tourist cruises and visited Spitsbergen annually, between 1906–1910. Such tours lasted four weeks, with the "Oceana" sailing from Hamburg to the Faeroe Islands and Iceland before visiting Spitsbergen and Norway. She undertook two voyages each summer, although she only managed one in 1908, probably due to an accident at Leith, in Scotland. The polar explorer Henry Bryant, who had been second in command of Peary's relief expedition, travelled on board the 1910 cruise. He noted that on 15

The "Oceana's" passengers at the summit of Nordkapp, 18th July 1909 (courtesy Norsk Folkemuseum).

143

"Oceana" – light shaft opening up the dining room area.

July the ship passed close to Jan Mayen and that good views were obtained of this remote and rarely seen Norwegian outpost. Surprisingly, Jan Mayen experiences on average only three clear days a year and to see the dramatic snowy slopes of Beerenberg, the island's 2,500-metre extinct volcano, was clearly an event worth recording. In 1911, HAPAG rebuilt the "Deutschland", its fast 16,505-ton steamship, and converted her into the world's largest cruise ship, accommodating 487 first-class passengers. She was renamed "Victoria Luise" and took over "Oceana's" schedule to Spitsbergen in 1912 and continued until 1914, when only one voyage was possible due to the outbreak of war.

The 16,339-ton steamship "Cincinnati" visited Spitsbergen in 1911, while the "Kronprinzessin Cecile", built by Fried Krupp AG Kiel, toured the island during the summer of 1911 and 1912. The first trip included visits to Scotland and Iceland, while in 1912 the route was more direct, travelling along Norway's coast. Her most distinguished passenger, Frederick Augustus III, the last King of Saxony, was so impressed with the 1911 tour that he made the ship's captain a Knight of the Albrecht Order. The 8,699-ton "Kronprinzessin Cecile", however, should not be confused with

Beerenberg, the volcanic summit of Jan Mayen, as seen by Henry Bryant in 1910.

the large "four stack liner", with the same name, that ran under the Norddeutscher Lloyd on the transatlantic route. Finally, the 8,332-ton "Fürst Bismark" visited Spitsbergen in 1913, although after being renamed "Friedrichsruh" in 1914, she was laid up at Hamburg and turned over to the British in 1919.

A 1907 flyer for the American market offering cruises to Norway, Iceland and Spitsbergen.

"Cincinnati's" route, 1911.

146

HAPAG's brochures for 1906, 1911, 1912 advertising cruises to Spitsbergen.

Norddeutscher Lloyd

HAPAG's main rival, Norddeutscher Lloyd (North German Lloyd), was established in 1857 in Bremen and rapidly grew to become one of the largest and most successful shipping businesses, having established its international reputation by prizing the "Blue Ribbon" from Cunard in 1897. Although the company's head office was located in Bremen, its passenger ships were berthed at Bremerhaven, a port that boasted the biggest dock system in the world and which was to become known as "Lloyd's Town". At the outbreak of the World War I, Norddeutscher Lloyd employed 26,000 people, of whom 15,000 worked onboard its 116 ships.

The company's first Spitsbergen cruise was in 1908, when the steamer "Grosser Kurfürst" visited the island's west coast. She was built by Schichau in Danzig in 1900 and at 13,812-ton and 177 metres in length was the largest of her class. Originally designed for the Imperial Mail Service to East Asia and Australia, she had the capacity to carry 144 first class, 281 second class and 2,373 steerage passengers. In the summer months, when there was limited business in the southern hemisphere, she cruised the Atlantic and visited Spitsbergen six times between 1908 and 1913. These cruises lasted approximately thirty days and included visits to France, Scotland, Iceland, Spitsbergen and Norway, before returning to Germany. The first tour spent a limited time in Spitsbergen, visiting only Bellsund and Adventfjorden, but in subsequent years the cruises became more adventurous, reaching as far afield as Raudfjorden on the north-west coast. Motorboats were used for landings in remote locations,

The "Grosser Kurfürst" anchored in Adventfjorden.

including Hamburgbukta, with its sixteenth century German whaling relics. Today's tourists, in contrast, are ferried ashore by rubber inflatables, although the difficulty of access to Hamburgbukta still limits the number of visitors.

The ability of the Norddeutscher Lloyd's cruises to reach such isolated fjords was the result of the experience gained from Count Zeppelin's expedition to Spitsbergen in the summer of 1910. The Count, ostensibly with the aim of experimenting with dirigible balloons for a North Pole attempt, set up base camp at Signehamna, in Krossfjorden. The expedition, which included Prince Heinrich of Prussia, had the free use of Norddeutscher Lloyd's luxurious liner "Mainz". The coastal area and bays along Spitsbergen's north-eastern corner were extensively explored and the results suggested that large vessels could safely negotiate the coastal channels as far as Raudfjorden. Expedition photographs were used to illustrate the company's promotional literature and encouraged many tourists to visit the area over the next few years. A meteorological station, which was established in Longyearbyen, was subsequently moved to Ebeltofthamna, on the west side of Krossfjorden and its small party of scientists was replaced annually. Max Dietrich, captain of the "Mainz", was subsequently appointed skipper of the "Grosser Kurfürst" and his valuable arctic experience contributed to the success

Early colour photograph by Miethe (1910) used by Norddeutscher Lloyd in its promotional literature.

Max Dietrich, captain of the "Mainz" (1910) and "Grosser Kurfürst" (1911–13).

of these pioneering cruises. Dietrich had an adventurous life. He ran away to sea at the age of seventeen and after gaining experience on several ships joined Norddeutscher Lloyd in 1901, to become the company's youngest captain. At the outbreak of war, the "Grosser Kurfürst", like a number of other German ships, was impounded in New York. Dietrich, however, managed to slip through the blockade and return to Germany for which he was awarded the "Iron Cross". It is likely that his encounters with Count Zeppelin during the 1910 "study trip" kindled an interest in airships and led him to transfer to the German Naval Airship Division. During the war, he commanded a number of Zeppelins until his death in 1916, when he was shot down over England's east coast during a bombing raid.

The Norddeutscher Lloyd's itinerary frequently included Regnardneset, a small beach at the head of Møllerfjorden, where beer tents were erected for beach parties and barbecues. This German tradition continued after the war and in 1926 a permanent hut was erected which became

Brochure advertising Spitsbergen cruise, 1911.

150

"Grosser Kurfürst's" menu, 28th July 1911. Note the photograph at top of menu could be detached and used as a postcard.

"Grosser Kurfürst's" passengers inspect a whale skeleton, Bellsund.

known as "Lloyd's Hotel". The "northernmost hotel in the world" still exists today and its continuing popularity with tourists can be judged by the number of signatures in its guest book. In 1911, the ice conditions were unfavourable and the "Grosser Kurfürst" was forced to spend more time than scheduled exploring the western fjords, including

The "Grosser Kürfurst's" tourists visit Wellman's camp on Danskøya.

Krossfjorden and Lilliehöökfjorden. In Möllerfjorden, two Norwegian hunters requested a passage home, together with their haul of seal and fox skins, eider down and birds eggs. They were members of a four-man party that had been sent to the area for two winters by a Tromsø-based company. Pages have been written about the adventures of such hardy and fearless individuals and the names of many have passed into folklore. Between 1900 and 1910, as many as two hundred trappers visited Spitsbergen, with many seeking assistance from tourist ships to transport stores, deliver mail or to provide a lift back to the mainland.

Adventfjorden was the final anchorage for tours after 1908 and the stopover provided an opportunity for visitors to explore the mine workings and purchase souvenirs from the legendary hunter, Klaus Thue. This passing trade must have been worthwhile, for Thue returned every summer for over ten years, pitching his tent on the shoreline, to sell postcards, fossils, whale teeth and skins. Cruise ships, however, were not always welcome, as access to alcohol frequently resulted in worker drunkenness. Longyear City's site manager successfully warned the "Grosser Kurfürst's" crew against landing alcohol or fire-arms. This was not always the case

"Grosser Kurfürst's" passengers disembarking at Möllerfjorden.

Tourists exploring the shore near the Waggonwaybreen's snout.

Tourists scrambling on the lower slopes of Gullybreen. Note the "Grosser Kurfürst" anchored in fjord (far right).

"Grosser Kurfürst" heading into Krossfjorden.

"Grosser Kurfürst's" tourists disembarking at Magalenefjorden.

Raudfjorden – the remotest fjord visted by "Grosser Kurfürst"

and when the VDS's vessel "Andenæs" arrived several days later, her officers failed to keep their promise. Many of the company's employees went aboard, including the doctor, and became intoxicated, while a number remained drunk for days after smuggling spirits ashore. The "Kong Harald" and "Neptun", which visited later in the season, caused a repetition of this nuisance and forced the management to take preventative measures.

An additional concern was the tourists' enthusiasm for souvenirs and keepsakes, which had already begun to have a detrimental effect on the island's historical sites. Indeed, by 1910 damage to Wellman's and Andrée's camps had been commented on and today neither building remains standing. Unfortunately, such activity continued unchecked and it was not until 1974 that regulations were introduced to protect the remaining relics. These measures are wide ranging and prohibit the destruction, removal, or defacement of any artefact of human activity that predates 1946.

Those on board the 1913 cruise would have been waiting anxiously for news of the German Schröder-Stranz Expedition, which had run into difficulties while wintering in Sorgfjorden. At the time, it was known that at least four

> **SCHROEDER-STRANZ SAFE?**
>
> **Wireless from Spitzbergen Seems to Indicate Explorer's Rescue.**
>
> BREMEN, July 23.—The rescue of the missing German Arctic explorer, Lieut. Schroeder-Stranz, is apparently indicated in a mangled wireless dispatch received here to-day from the steamer Grosser Kurfürst, which is cruising in Spitzbergen waters. The message is as follows:
>
> Dr. Robitzsch of the German Observatory at Cross Bay came on board yesterday at Moeller Bay and made important communications about Schroeder-Stranz. Help has been received. A detailed report will be sent by wireless from Tromsoe.
>
> The Grosser Kurfürst is due at Tromsoe on Friday.

New York Times, 24ᵗʰ July 1913.

of its members had died and that the leader and ten others had also probably perished. However, whilst visiting Möllerfjorden, the "Grosser Kurfürst" welcomed onboard a member of the German meteorological station who incorrectly reported that Schröder-Stranz was alive. A message containing this false information was radioed from the ship and avidly reported by the world's press. It remains unclear whether this was a genuine misunderstanding, or "spin" on part of the Germans to mask the expedition's incompetence. It may be relevant that Germany had territorial ambitions for Spitsbergen and had already laid claim to the area around Ebeltofhamna.

The following summer, Norddeutscher Lloyd sent the 17,802-ton cruise ship "Prinz Freidrich Wilhelm" to

A tourist cabin, "Prinz Freidrich Wilhelm".

Spitsbergen, together with Ebeltofhamna's relief party for the winter of 1914/15. However, while *en route* from Iceland to Spitsbergen, Austria-Hungary declared war on Serbia, an event that led to the conflict now known as World War I. As a result, "Prinz Friedrich Wilhelm", which had only just reached Spitsbergen, was ordered to return promptly to Germany to avoid being cut off, or sunk, by the Royal Navy. Her hasty departure, however, meant that the scheduled visit to Ebeltofhamna was abandoned and the German meteorologists were left to their fate. Fortunately, the three men eventually found a passage home, although a visiting Norwegian tourist ship declined to help in order to maintain an attitude of neutrality. The "Prinz Friedrich Wilhelm" reached Norway without incident and anchored in Puddefjorden, near Bergen, where the passengers and most of the crew were put ashore to make their own way home. The captain with a skeleton crew of forty, then moved the ship to Odda, where she remained until 1916 before eventually making a run for Kiel, where she was laid up until the war ended.

The German steamship companies ended the war with most of their ships either seized by the Allies, or bottled up by the British blockade. Furthermore, under the Treaty of Versailles, Germany was required to give up all vessels greater than 1,600 tons, a fact that effectively put an end to this early phase of German tourism. After the "Grosser Kurfürst" was seized, she was renamed "City of Los Angeles" and placed on the Hawaiian run, where she proved a popular vessel with Hollywood stars and wealthy businessmen. The "Prinz Friedrich Wilhelm", however, was

"Prinz Friedrich Wilhelm's" planned itinerary, 1914.

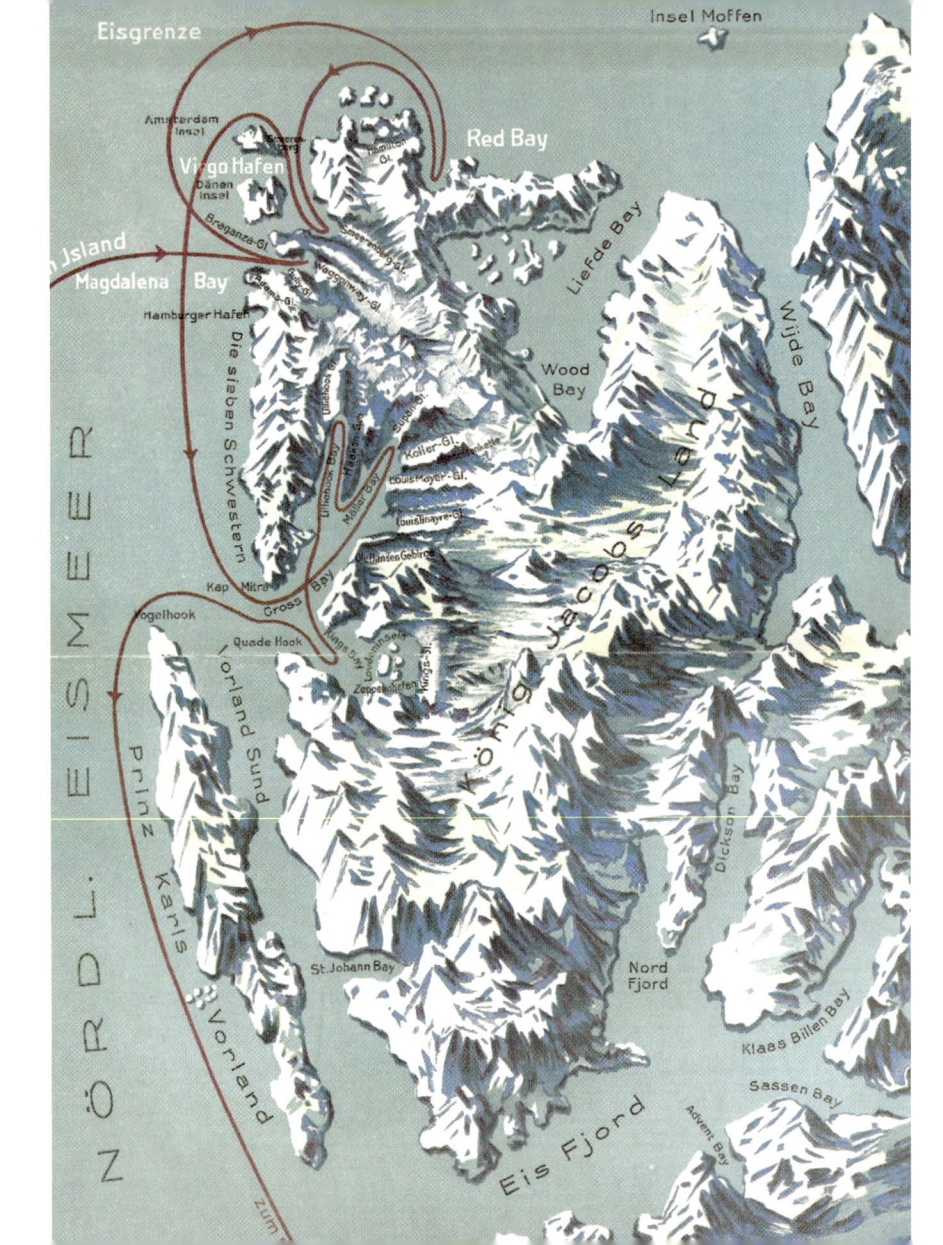

ceded to the British in 1920 as war reparation and after being refitted and renamed several times was sold to the Canadian Pacific Line. Norddeutscher Lloyd's maritime operations did not recommence for a further eight years, although continued until 1970, when it amalgamated with the Hamburg-Amerika-Linie to become the HAPAG-Lloyd group of today.

Germany's territorial ambitions

In 1912, Norddeutscher Lloyd, in conjunction with Prince Heinrich of Prussia, Ferdinand von Zeppelin, Professor Hergesell and the Deutscher Seefisherei-Verein (German Sea Fishery Organisation), set about claiming tracts of land along Spitsbergen's coastline in the name of Germany. Initially, five kilometres around Tinayrebukta, a small bay on the east side of Krossfjorden, was claimed, as significant coal deposits had been discovered in the area. Further claims were made around Hamburgbukta and Magdalenefjorden, where boards were erected with the inscriptions, *"Eigentum des Norddeutscher Lloyd, Bremen, Germany"* (Property of Norddeuscher Lloyd, Bremen, Germany). During the next two years, the company's agent made use of visits by the

Route map for the "Grosser Kurfürst's" 1912 cruise.

"Grosser Kurfürst" and "Prinz Friedrich Wilhelm" to erect further boards around Möllerfjorden, Raudfjorden and Magdalenefjorden. All these claims were formally lodged with the German Ministry of Foreign Affairs under the title, "Land Protection Register for Land Requirements on Spitsbergen and Bjørnøya".

The outbreak of international hostilities, however, put an end to Germany's territorial plans and her many claims were never pursued. Nevertheless, the continuing international interest in Spitsbergen, resulting from the various economic activities on the island, made it imperative that the issue of sovereignty was clarified. This pressing need led to the Treaty of Svalbard, signed on 9 February 1920, which gave Norway sovereignty over the islands, an arrangement that continues to the present day.

Areas claimed by Germany 1912–1914. Norddeutscher Lloyd (horizontal lines), Graf Zeppelin and Hugo Hergesell (hatched lines), Prinz Heinrich of Prussia (black shading). (from Hoel).

French Cruises

Ile-de-France

The increasing popularity of Spitsbergen as a holiday destination was reflected in the fact that at least eight tourist vessels visited the island during the summer of 1906. They included the first French ship, the 3,488-ton "Ile-de-France", in a venture organised by the Compagnie des Transports Maritimes à Vapeur, in conjunction with the Revue Générale des Sciences (General Review of Sciences). The cruise, led by the eminent Swedish geologist Nils Otto Nordenskiöld, cost 1,850 francs and offered visitors a scientific introduction to the unique geography of the high arctic. A supplement of 400 francs was charged for those wishing to join the various hunting trips (e.g. for whale, reindeer, fox and seal) and covered the hire of a whaler and her crew, onshore guides, horses, tents and weapons. The "Ile-de-France" was undoubtedly one of the best fitted out vessels of her day, as evidenced by the following account from the tour's promotional literature:

Nils Otto Nordenskiöld, a Swedish geologist, geographer and leader of the 1906 tour. He had considerable polar experience, having led the Swedish Antarctic Expedition, 1901–1903.

For her tonnage and dimensions, the ship's facilities exceed that of many luxury yachts. There is accommodation for 214 tourists in roomy cabins, of which 42 have a single bed, 71 with two beds and 10 with three beds (there are no bunk beds). Each cabin is furnished with a large washbasin for each person, a chest of drawers, a cupboard, coat pegs, a sizable mirror, shelves, a desk, a cane bench, a chair for each person, two lamps, an electric ventilator and an adjustable heater. The ship is lit by electric lights throughout and is equipped with central heating, which in winter is sufficient to keep all the cabins, rooms and corridors warm. The ship has seven bathrooms, each of which is provided with a shower. There are two salons on the upper deck; the largest of which seats 184 diners, while the smaller one serves as a lounge, used especially for women. Men, therefore, are invited to use it with discretion and only when there is room. A spacious smoking room, also located on the upper deck, provides a meeting place for men. There is a large open space at the back of the upper deck where tourists can set out their deck-chairs and where there is shelter in case of bad weather. In order to ensure the speed and safety of embarking and disembarking, the "Ile-de-France" carries a steamer of 35 horse-power, which can simultaneously tow all the launches.

The tour departed from Dunkirk in July, with one hundred and eighty-four passengers, including the artists, Felix Fournery and Emile Gallois, the writer René Bazin, the photographer Paul Grenot and the legendary cameraman Emile Lauste. After steaming across the North Sea and along the Norwegian coast, she reached Lofoten on Bastille Day, where her passengers mingled with those of the "Neptun" for celebratory drinks. At Tromsø, horses and Norwegian hunters were taken on board, together with Johan Kjeldsen, an experienced ice-pilot, whose role was to ensure the safety of the ship as she navigated through the ever shifting ice floes. Forty-eight hours later, she entered Recherchefjorden and anchored alongside several Norwegian whaling vessels and the German tourist liner, "Oceana". Next day, hunting parties were put ashore in Adventdalen and Sassendalen, while other passengers explored the American coal mine at Longyear City. The cruise then proceeded to Virgohamna, with the opportunity to visit Wellman's base camp. Indeed, Emile Lauste, working as cameraman for the Charles Urban Trading Company,

Johan Kjeldsen acted as ice-pilot for the "Ile-de-France" (1906), as well as for the "Pallas" (1881) and "Grosser Kurfürst" (1908). He discovered and named Kvitøya in 1874 and achieved international fame for his heroic rescue of Zachariassen, who had became stranded on Spitsbergen in 1901.

The memorial cairn, whose construction detained "Friesland".

made a short, but historically important film of Wellman's activities, which can be found today in the British National Film and Television Archives.

Across the bay, the cruiser "Friesland" would have been in full view. She had been sent by the Dutch government to collect the skeletons of the seventeenth and eighteenth century whalers that littered the surrounding area and to give them a formal burial. The recovered bones, including all those from the islands, Likholmen and Amsterdamøya, were amassed and placed in a large tumulus, on top of which was built a memorial cairn. This activity took much longer than originally planned and the resultant delay enabled the "Friesland" to play a crucial role in the rescue of the "Ile-de-France", several days later.

After leaving Virgohamna, the French captain, lured on by the remarkably favourable weather and ice conditions, took the "Ile-de-France" into Raudfjorden, a remote and rarely visited fjord on the north coast. Suddenly, at 8 o'clock in the morning, the vessel shuddered to a grinding halt, having hit a submerged rock near the fjord's entrance. As the tide turned, she began to list dangerously and orders were given to jettison her ballast, together with fifty tons of coal reserves. Unfortunately, this manoeuvre had little effect and the ship was left stranded in a precarious and exposed position. Clearly, if a sudden storm had arisen, or dense fog had prevented their plight from being discovered, then loss of life could have ensued.

"Ile-de-France" aground and listing off Raudfjorden.

Fortunately, the German journalist and explorer, Theodore Lerner, was in the vicinity in his chartered steamer "Express", having been sent by a German newspaper to cover Wellman's North Pole Expedition. The construction of Wellman's hangar took much longer than expected and the American adventurer was forced to postpone his attempt until the following year. With time on his hands, Lerner decided to undertake a hunting trip along the north coast and it was while off Raudfjorden that he spotted "Ile-de-France's" distress signals. The twelve-ton "Express", however, lacked the necessary power to pull her free and after

Theodor Lerner (1866–1931)

164

The "Express" chartered by Lerner.

"Ile-de-France's" tourists being ferried ashore to await rescue, 1906.

Gold chronometer presented to Lerner by the passengers of the "Ile-de-France", 1906.

Chronometer case entitled, "To Theodor Lerner. Grateful compliments from the passengers of the "Ile-de-France".

several failed attempts was despatched to locate the more powerful "Friesland". The Dutch ship was located nearby, in Liefdefjorden, although by the time she returned most of the French tourists, fearing that their ship would sink, had been ferried ashore with a limited supply of food and water. At high tide the following day, the "Ile-de-France" was successfully re-floated and soon her passengers were back onboard, shouting, "Vivre Lerner! Vivre la Hollande". A collection of approximately thirteen thousand Francs was donated to the crew and some months later Lerner was sent an inscribed gold pocket chronometer in appreciation of his role in the rescue.

That this was the only serious accident in the pioneering days of Spitsbergen cruises was remarkable. Indeed, even today, with modern navigational aids, cruising in such an environment is not without risk. In 1989, for example, the 630-foot, Soviet tourist ship "Maxim Gorky" hit an iceberg while cruising off north-west Spitsbergen and suffered three large holes below the waterline. Her passengers were forced to take to the life-boats, although in contrast to 1906, everyone was carried to safety within hours by helicopter.

The second cruise organised by the General Review of Sciences was in 1910, under the leadership of the polar explorers, Oscar Backlund and Henryk Arctowski. Backlund was an authority on Spitsbergen, while Arctowski had served on the scientific staff of Gerlache's Antarctic Expedition of 1897–1899 and was experienced in geology, oceanography and meteorology. The "Ile-de-France" was chartered again, although this time the party was smaller, with only eighty-eight tourists. Seven days out of Dunkirk, they arrived at Tromsø and rendezvoused with

Oscar Backlund, co-leader of the 1910 cruise, studied astronomy at Uppsala University and was a member of the Swedish-Russian Arc-of-Meridian expedition in Spitsbergen, 1898–1902.

the "Viking", a small steam ship that would accompany the cruise for safety. After a brief visit to Adventfjorden, the "Ile-de-France" entered Templefjorden, with its spectacular mountains and impressive glacial scenery. Hunting parties, equipped for several days, were put ashore, while others explored the area around von Postbreen, Skansbukta and the coastal mountains to the south of Sassenfjorden. A small party made the third ascent of Marmierfjellet, a 709-metre mountain, while nearby four peaks were named in the cruise's honour; Roulletegga, Oliviertoppen, Ile-de-Francekollen and Arctowskifjellet. Finally, as dense pack-ice blocked the entrance to Raudfjorden, the two vessels headed north, with the *Viking* reaching 80° 5'N.

Advertisement for a "Cruise in the Polar Word. Norway, Spitsbergen and the Pack-Ice", 1910.

167

The "Viking" at Grønfjorden, 1910.

Climbing party setting off from Sassendalen, 1910.

...he third ascent of Marmierfjellet, 1910.

Passengers enjoying refreshments off Spitsbergen, 1910.

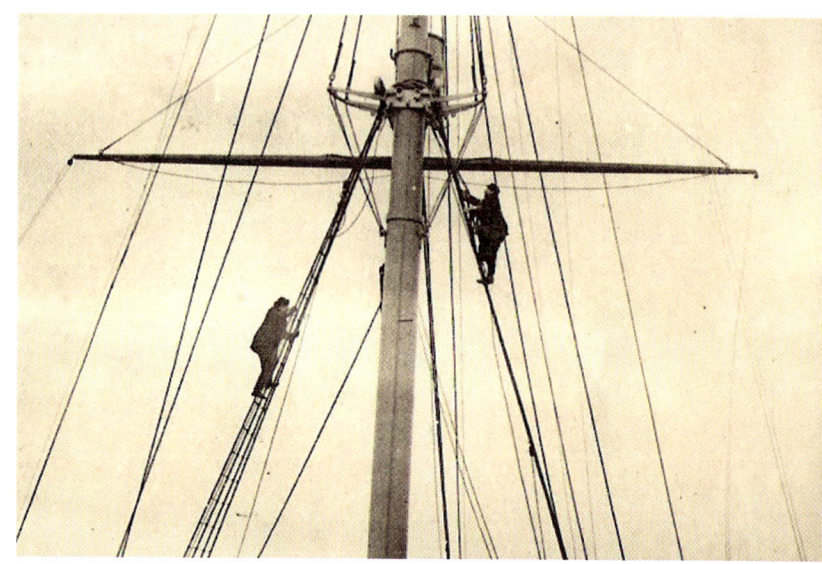

"Ile-de-France" and "Viking" at Camp Wellman, 1910. The hangar was rebuilt with nine arches in 1909 after the five arch structure collapsed during the winter, 1906/07.

Seeking a route through the ice, 1910.

The "Viking" departing for the pack-ice, 1910.

Postcards as Snapshots in History

Whilst the handwritten postcard can reveal tantalising insights into the daily lives of the first tourists, the accompanying illustrations provide us with valuable snapshots of the island's early history. A variety of subjects were offered by the early publishers, including scenes of the coal mining settlements, hunting trips, exploration and mapping of the island's interior, the whale fishery, the tourist hotel and the North Pole expeditions of Andrée and Wellman.

Coal Mining and Settlements

The sloop "Gottfried". The sealing captain Zachariassen was the first to mine coal commercially. In 1862, after being shipwrecked near Kapp Bohemann, he discovered an exposed coal seam. Returning in 1899 in the "Gottfried", Zachariassen mined a cargo of coal and sold it, partly to the tourist hotel at Adventfjorden and partly on mainland Norway.

Advent City, the world's northernmost town. The Spitsbergen Coal and Trading Company of Sheffield commenced mining on the eastern shore of Adventfjorden in 1904. To support their activities a settlement was constructed, consisting of a dozen well-built cabins, that included a store and bakery.

Advent City boasted the first women and horses to be resident in a Spitsbergen mining settlement, 1906. At its busiest, 100 men were employed, although only one or two vessels were coaled every summer and exports never exceeded two thousand tons a year.

Advent City's post office. The mine was not a success, due to competition from the more profitable seams around Longyear City, and was abandoned after a few years.

Longyear City under construction. The first building was constructed in 1906 and by 1910 the settlement housed 200 men.

Longyear City's concrete barracks were partitioned into four-man bays with communal washing basins and ovens at the end of a central corridor.

In 1907, a strong jetty (Gamlekaia, or "old wharf") was built that extended 180 metres out from the shore, along which colliers could load. The tourist vessel "Neptun" can be seen at anchor.

The "William D. Munro", named after Longyear's cousin, transported building material needed for Longyear City's construction.

Hunting

Reindeer were keenly sought after by the early tourist hunting parties.

Exploration and Mapping of Spitsbergen's interior

The systematic surveying and mapping of Spitsbergen's interior was initiated by Gunnar Isachsen in 1906. The picture shows the upper reaches of Fjortende Julibreen, photographed by Isachsen 10th August 1906.

The Whale Fishery

Whalers in Bellsund. The 282-foot "Bucentaur" was converted to a factory ship in 1904 and sent to the Spitsbergen fishery for the seasons 1905–07. The venture was backed by the Norwegian Joh H. Giæver and the Swiss chocolate magnate, Carl Suchard. Later, "Bucentaur" was transferred to the Southern Whale Fishery, based at South Georgia.

The "Kong Harald" visits the whaling station in Bellsund.

Whaling, Grønfjorden. A whaler with a string of blue and fin whales that have been inflated with air to maintain buoyancy.

Whaling Station, Grønfjorden. The smell of processing of whales drove Gerard to write, "*it permeates the printed page of your book; it nauseates your food; it taints your dreams; and it percolates your prayers*".

Tourist Hotel

A whale catch being towed to Grønfjorden for processing with an attendant raft of fulmars and gulls.

The prefabricated tourist hotel, or lodge, was erected by the Vesteraalens Dampskibsselskab in 1896 and was used during the summer months, 1896–1898.

"Tourist Hotel – the world's northernmost Post office". Note the external stairs that were added during the second season.

The hotel (centre left) was moved to Longyear City in 1908, were it was used as a storeroom and shop until its destruction by the German battleship "Tirpitz" in 1943, along with the rest of the settlement.

Andrée's North Pole Expedition

Andrée's prefabricated, wooden balloon hangar was erected on the shores of Danskøya in 1896.

The hydrogen generator required to inflate the balloon. The apparatus produced gas by the action of sulphuric acid, diluted with water, on iron filings. During the first twenty-four hours approximately 1,200 cubic metres of hydrogen was produced.

Wellman's North Pole Expedition.

Andrée's expedition vessels "Svensksund" and "Virgo" anchored off Virgohamna, 1897. The gun boat "Svensksund" was placed at Andrée's disposal by the Swedish Government and transported the balloon and gas producing apparatus. The remaining equipment and provisions were sent in the cargo vessel "Virgo".

Camp Wellman under construction in 1906. Wellman's expedition vessel "Frithjof" is at anchor in Virgohamna, together with three Norwegian tourist vessels; "Kong Harald", "Express" and "Neptun".

The expedition ship "Frithjof" carried not only hundreds of tons of timber and iron for the hangar and ancillary buildings, but also 125 tons of sulphuric acid and 75 tons of iron filings which, when combined with 30 tons of added chemicals, produced the required amount of hydrogen.

Tourists inspecting the motor engines of "America", the latter enabling the airship to proceed at a rate of 18 miles an hour for over 120 hours.

Camp Wellman in 1909, with Pike's house, used by Andrée, at front right.

The final hangar was built of nine arches fashioned on the spot, bent and bolted together on bending frames and covered with nearly an acre of strong canvas.

Isachsen's survey vessel "Farm" comes to the rescue of the "America" after its short-lived flight, August 1909.

Appendix A
Tourist Stamps (Etiquettes)

A series of Spitsbergen etiquettes (stamps) were issued for tourist use and, except for the "Spidsbergen" 10 and 20 øre, had no postal value and were not recognised by receiving countries. After a German protest in 1897, however, even the "Spidsbergen" issues were not accepted and all etiquettes had to be used in combination with regular Norwegian stamps. Nevertheless, such decorative souvenirs became very popular and most visiting ships offered etiquettes for sale. The numbering and dates are as published in *Katalog over Norges Byposter*, 2005 by B. Schøyen and F. Aune.

Spidsbergen 1–2

Issued by the Vesteraalens Dampskibsselskap (VDS) in Stokmarknes in May 1896 and held in the hotel at Adventfjorden. They were sold to the visiting tourists by Emil Ellingsen and were the only "tourist stamps" officially recognised by the Norwegian Post Office.

Etiquette E1

Printed in Germany at the request of Captain Wilhelm Bade, to his own design, in 1897. One thousand copies were printed and they were used exclusively by tourists on Bade's cruises between 1897 and 1902.

Etiquette E3

Printed in Germany in 1898 (E2 was printed in 1897 using a slightly different plate) for Bade's cruises. They were popular with tourists as souvenirs and were probably printed in greater numbers than E1, with use being recorded up until 1902.

The 10 pfennig valued etiquettes are often found cancelled according to the destination visited, for example "Eisfjord", "Smeerenburg", "Magdalena Bai" and "Nordküste".

Etiquettes E4–E11

Set of three etiquettes (5, 10 and 20 øre), depicting polar bear, walrus and hunter in an arctic landscape. They were printed between 1897–1909, using three different plates, and issued by the Tromsø-based agent, Johannes Holmboe Giæver. They were widely used by the main shipping lines throughout the twelve year period.

which acted a post office for that year only. Steamships from the Hamburg-Amerika-Linie and Norddeutscher Lloyd would have used E4–E11 and would not have required the use of E13.

Etiquette E12–13

E12 is attributed to Giæver and was used by Hamburg-Amerika-Linie from 1898. E13 was probably issued in 1905 and used by the P&O steamer "Vectis" and may have been available in Recherchefjorden (1907) from Giæver's house,

Etiquette E14

Remainders of the 1896 issue were reused in 1906, after being overprinted with a hand struck '5 øre'. Primarily used by "Neptun" in 1906.

Etiquette E15–18

A series of four etiquettes issued over a six-year period from 1907–1913; 1907-blue (E15), 1908-red (E16), 1910-green (E17), 1913-purple (E18). Carried on board the Öesterreichischer Lloyd's steamship "Thalia", with the majority being posted to Germany and Austria.

Etiquette 21–23

Printed in 1909 and available on board Bergenske Dampskibsselskab ships as well as the Nordenfjeldske Dampskibsselskap ships between 1909 and 1912.

Etiquettes E24–32

Nine distinct etiquettes with values from 5 to 50 øre printed in 1911. They were widely used by the Norddeutscher Lloyd cruises and are found on most postcards from the "Grosser Kurfürst", as well as rare postcards from the "Prinz Friedrich Wilhelm" dated 1914.

Etiquettes E33–37

Four etiquettes, valued 5 to 50 öre, with polar bear facing left and one valued 1 Krone with fjord scene with bear and boat. All are rare and their use appears to have been restricted to the Hamburg-Amerika Linie in 1913.

Appendix B

Spitsbergen's Tourist Ships (1881–1914)

Year	Vessel	Shipping Company (Leader)
1881	Pallas	Bergenske Dampskibsselskab (H. Clodius)
1884	Ceylon	Orient Steam Navigation Company
1891	Amely	Droste, Gehrels & Comp. (W. Bade)
1893	Columbia	Hamburg-Amerika-Linie
	Admiral	Deutschen Öst-Afrika Linie (W. Bade)
1894	Lusitania	Orient Steam Navigation Company
	Stettin	Norddeutscher Lloyd (W. Bade)
1895	Columbia	Hamburg-Amerika-Linie
	Danzig	Norddeutscher Lloyd (W. Bade)
1896	Columbia	Hamburg-Amerika-Linie
	Garonne	Orient Steam Navigation Company

	Lofoten	Vesteraalen Dampskibsselskab
	Erling Jarl	Bergenske Dampskibsselskab (W. Bade)
1897	Auguste Victoria	Hamburg-Amerika-Linie
	Garonne	Orient Steam Navigation Company
	Kong Harald	Nordenfjeldske Dampskibsselskab (W. Bade)
	Lofoten	Vesteraalen Dampskibsselskab
1898	Auguste Viktoria	Hamburg-Amerika-Linie
	Kong Harald	Nordenfjeldske Dampskibsselskab (W. Bade)
	Lofoten	Vesteraalen Dampskibsselskab
1899	Auguste Viktoria	Hamburg-Amerika- Linie
	Kong Harald	Nordenfjeldske Dampskibsselskab (W. Bade)
	Ophir	Orient Steam Navigation Company
	Lofoten	Vesteraalen Dampskibsselskab
1900	Auguste Victoria	Hamburg-Amerika-Linie
	Hertha	A/S Oceana, Sandefjord (W. Bade)
	Cuzco	Orient Steam Navigation Company
1901	Auguste Victoria	Hamburg-Amerika-Linie

1902	Oihonna	Finska Ångfartygs A/B (W. Bade)
	Auguste Victoria	Hamburg-Amerika-Linie
	Mexic	Orient Steam Navigation Company
1903	Oihonna	Finska Angfartygs A/B (A. Bade)
	Auguste Victoria	Hamburg-Amerika-Linie
	Prinzessin Victoria Luise	Hamburg-Amerika-Linie
	Ophir	Orient Steam Navigation Company
1904	Oihoona	Finska Ångfartygs A/B (A. Bade)
	Prinzessin Victoria Luise	Hamburg-Amerika-Linie
	Blücher	Hamburg-Amerika-Linie
	Ophir	Orient Steam Navigation Company
1905	Oihonna	Finska Ångfartygs A/B (A. Bade)
	Moltke	Hamburg-Amerika-Linie
	Prinzessin Victoria Luise	Hamburg-Amerika-Linie
	Vectis	P & O Line
1906	Neptun	Bergenske Dampskibsselskab
	Ile-de-France	Cie G^{le} Transatlantique

	Oihonna	Finska Ångfartygs A/B (A. Bade)
	Prinzessin Victoria Luise	Hamburg-Amerika-Linie
	Blücher	Hamburg-Amerika-Linie
	Oceana	Hamburg-Amerika-Linie
	Kong Harald	Nordenfjeldske Dampskibsselskab
	Vectis	P & O Line
1907	Neptun	Bergenske Dampskibsselskab
	Blücher	Hamburg-Amerika-Linie
	Kronprinzessin Cecile	Hamburg-Amerika-Linie
	Oceana	Hamburg-Amerika-Linie
	Kong Harald	Nordenfjeldske Dampskibsselskab
	Thalia	Österreichischen Lloyd (A. Bade)
	Vectis	P & O Line
1908	Neptun	Bergenske Dampskibsselskab
	Kong Harald	Nordenfjeldske Dampskibsselskab
	Blücher	Hamburg-Amerika-Linie
	Oceana	Hamburg-Amerika-Linie

	Grosser Kurfürst	Norddeutscher Lloyd
	Thalia	Österreichischen Lloyd
	Vectis	P & O Line
	Andenæs	Vesteraalen Dampskipsselskab (A. Bade)
1909	Neptun	Bergenske Dampskibsselskab
	Blücher	Hamburg-Amerika-Linie
	Oceana	Hamburg-Amerika-Linie
	Kong Harald	Nordenfjeldske Dampskibsselskab
	Thalia	Österreichischen Lloyd
	Vectis	P & O Line
1910	Neptun	Bergenske Dampskibsselkab
	Ile-de-France	Cie G^{le} Transatlantique
	Blücher	Hamburg-Amerika-Linie
	Oceana	Hamburg-Amerika-Linie
	Kong Harald	Nordenfjeldske Dampskibsselskab
	Grosser Kurfürst	Norddeutscher Lloyd
	Thalia	Österreichischen Lloyd

	Vectis	P & O Line
1911	Neptun	Bergenske Dampskibsselskab
	Cincinnati	Hamburg-Amerika-Linie
	Oceana	Hamburg-Amerika-Linie
	Blücher	Hamburg-Amerika-Linie
	Kronprinzessin Cecile	Hamburg-Amerika-Linie
	Grosser Kurfürst	Norddeutscher Lloyd
	Kong Harald	Nordenfjeldske Dampskibsselskab
	Vectis	P & O Line
	Andenæs	Vesteraalen Dampskibsselskab
1912	Vega	Bergenske Dampskibsselskab
	Kronprinzessin Cecile	Hamburg-Amerika-Linie
	Victoria Luise	Hamburg-Amerika-Linie
	Grosser Kurfürst	Norddeutscher Lloyd
	Kong Harald	Nordenfjeldske Dampskibsselskab
	Vectis	P & O Line
	Andenæs	Vesteraalen Dampskibsselskab

1913	Vega	Bergenske Dampskibsselskab
	Victoria Luise	Hamburg-Amerika-Linie
	Fürst Bismark	Hamburg-Amerika-Linie
	Grosser Kurfürst	Norddeutscher Lloyd
	Kong Harald	Nordenfjeldske Dampskibsselskab
	Thalia	Österreichischen Lloyd
	Vectis	P & O Line
	Andenæs	Vesteraalen Dampskibsselskab
1914	Neptun	Bergenske Dampskibsselskab
	Victoria Luise	Hamburg-Amerika-Linie
	Prinz Friedrich Wilhelm	Norddeutscher Lloyd
	Kong Harald	Nordenfjeldske Dampskibsselskab

SHIPS' POSTCARDS

Bergenske Dampskibsselskap (BDS)

Neptun (1906–1911, 1914). *A 959-ton vessel, built by Joh. C. Tecklenborg, Greestemünde in 1890, was scrapped 1928.*

Vega (1912–1913). *A 1,166-ton vessel, built by Joseph L. Thompson & Sons, Sunderland in 1895. She accompanied "Kong Harald" for two summers only and was lost in thew war in 1916.*

Cie de Transport Maritime à Vapeur

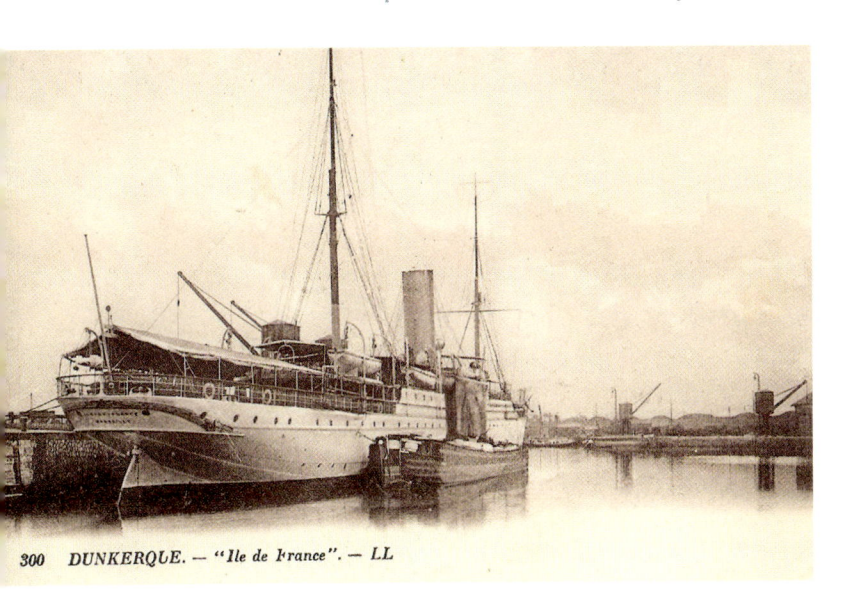

Ile-de-France (1906, 1910). *The 3,488-ton steamship, built by J. Elder & Co., Glasgow in 1882, was scrapped in 1915.*

Finska Ångfartygs Aktiebolaget

Oihonna (1902–1906). *The 1,076-ton vessel, built by Gourlay Brothers, Dundee in 1898, was chartered by Wilhelm and Axel Bade before being scrapped in 1960.*

Hamburg-Amerika-Linie

Columbia (1893, 1895–1896). *The 7,365-ton vessel was the first of the Hamburg-Amerika-Linie ships to visit Spitsbergen. She was built by Laird Brothers, Birkenhead in 1889 and sold to the Russians in 1904.*

Auguste Victoria (1897–1903). *The 7,661-ton steamship was built by A.G.Vulcan, Stettin in 1889 as the "Augusta Victoria" until correctly renamed after her refit at Harland and Wolff, Belfast in June 1897. She was sold to Russia in 1904.*

Prinzessin Victoria Luise (1903–1906). Built by Blohm & Voss in 1900 as a pleasure yacht, she visited Spitsbergen annually from 1903 until she was lost on a sandbank off Jamaica in 1906.

Blücher (1904, 1906–1911). The 12,334-ton vessel was delivered to the Hamburg-Amerika-Linie by Blohm & Voss in 1902. A sister ship to "Moltke", she was 168 metres long and powered by two screws giving a speed of 15.5 knots. In 1912, after being rebuilt and having luxurious new suites added on her boat deck, she entered the South American service before being eventually scrapped at Genoa in 1929.

***Moltke* (1905).** *The 12,335-ton sister ship to the "Blücher" was built by Blohm & Voss in 1901. She visited Spitsbergen only once and was eventually seized by Italy in 1915.*

***Moltke*'s Grill Room.** *The "Grill Room" showing the high level of furnishings characteristic of the age. The "Moltke" was transferred to the Genoa-New York run in 1906, interned in Genoa at the outbreak of World War I, confiscated by Italy in 1915 and scrapped there in 1915.*

Oceana (1906–1910). *Built by William Denny & Brothers, Dumbarton, in 1891, the 7,859-ton vessel was originally the Union Line "Scot" until 1905. She visited Spitsbergen twice a year, except for 1908 when she made only one voyage.*

Kronprinzessin Cecile (1911–1912). *The 8,688-ton, 6,700hp steamship was built in 1906 and ploughed the trans-Atlantic route to Cuba and Mexico. With a length of 143 metres, she was able to carry 1,228 passengers and 200 officers and crew.*

***Cincinnati* (1911)** *The 17,000-ton, twin-screwed, "Cincinnati" was built by F. Schichau of Danzig and launched on July 14th 1908. With a cruising speed of 15.5 knots, she could accommodate 300 first class, 350 second class and almost 1900 steerage class passengers while on the North Atlantic route. She lay in Boston in 1914, was confiscated by the United States and used as a troop transporter in 1917 as the "Covington", before being sunk by a German U-boat (U-86) in the Atlantic off the French coast in 1918.*

***Victoria Luise* (1912–1914).** *A 16,502-ton steamship, built by A.G. Vulcan, Stettin in 1900 as the "Deutschland". In 1911, she was rebuilt as the "Victoria Luise" to become the largest cruise ship in the world, before being scrapped in 1925.*

Norddeutscher Lloyd

Fürst Bismarck (1913). The 8,338-ton, 148-metre long steamship was built by Fairfield Shipbuilding and Engineering Company, Glasgow, in 1905. She went into HAPAG passenger and freight service from Hamburg to Cuba and Mexico in 1906. After being renamed "Friedrichsruh" in 1914, she was laid up in Hamburg and eventually turned over to the British in 1919 as war reparations.

Grosser Kurfürst (1908–1913). A 13,182-ton, twin-screw, steamer, built in 1900 by F. Schichau, Danzig. She was 177 metres in length and had a capacity of 144 first class, 281 second class and 2,373 steerage class passengers. She was named after Frederich William, the "Great Elector" (Grosser Kurfürst) who ruled Brandenberg from 1640-81.

Nordenfjeldske Dampskibsselskap NDS)

Prinz Friedrich Wilhelm (1914). *The 17,082-ton steamship, built by Joh. C. Tecklenborg, Geestemünde in 1908, was one of the last cruise ships to sail for Spitsbergen before the outbreak of World War I. She was ordered to return to Germany on arrival, however, and after the war, she was renamed "Montnairn" and sold to the Canadian Pacific Line.*

Erling Jarl (1896). *The 677-ton "Erling Jarl" was built by Trondhjems Mek. Verk., in 1895. She was refitted in 1909 and totally lost in 1941.*

Orient Steam Navigation Company

Kong Harald (1906–1914). *The 953-ton "Kong Harald" was built by Joh. C. Tecklenborg, Geestemünde in 1890 and carried approximately 100 passengers. She was scrapped in 1951.*

Ceylon (1884). *The 2,186-ton vessel was built by Samuda Brothers, London in 1858 and scrapped in 1907. She was privately owned for many years and undertook the Polytechnic cruises to Norway in the 1890's.*

Ophir (1899, 1903–1904). A 6,910-ton vessel, built for the Orient Pacific Line by R. Napier & Sons, Glasgow in 1891, was scrapped in 1922.

Österreichischen Lloyd

Thalia (1907–1913). The 2,371-ton vessel was owned by the Österreichischen Lloyd (Austrian Lloyd) and built by W. Denny & Brothers, Dumbarton, in 1886. She was refitted and converted to a saloon ship for luxurious cruises in 1907 and visited Spitsbergen annually between 1907–1913. She was scrapped in 1926.

Pacific and Orient Line (P&O)

Vectis (1905–1912). *The 5,545-ton ship was built by Caird & Co., Greenock, Scotland, in 1881 as the "Rome". She was sold soon after her final cruise to Spitsbergen in 1912.*

Appendix C
Explanation of Place-Names

The Norwegian spelling of Spitsbergen's place-names has been used throughout this book, as those used in primary material vary confusingly and their inclusion would have made the text difficult to follow (the exception being primary sources that have been quoted verbatim). The following list contains all the place-names referred to in this book, with an explanation of their origins (adapted from *The Place Names of Svalbard*. Norsk Polarinstitutt 2003).

(The addition in brackets gives the word with the definite article)

bre(en)	glacier	hamn(a)	harbour
bukt(a)	bay	haug(en)	hill
by(en)	town	huk(en)	headland
dal(en)	valley	nes(et)	point
fjell(et)	mountain	odde(n)	point, cape
fjord (en)	fjord	strand(a)	strand, shore
fonn(a)	snowfield	sund(et)	strait sound
gruve (gruva)	mine	våg (en)	protected bay
halvøy(a)	peninsula	øy(a)	island

Activekammen	-	a mountain between Dunderbukta and Recherchefjorden, after the iron corvette "Active" which visited the area in 1895.
Adambreen	-	a small glacier on the south side of Magdalenefjorden
Advent City	-	deserted mining camp on the east side of Adventfjorden, built by the Spitzbergen Coal and Trading Company Limited of Sheffield 1904 and 1905.
Adventdalen	-	large, open valley running in a southeasterly direction and easterly direction from the head of Adventfjorden.
Adventfjorden	-	named after the British whaler "Adventure" which was stationed in Isfjorden in 1656.
Adventpynten	-	low sandy point on Hotellneset.
Akseløya	-	island separating Bellsund and Van Mijenfjorden, named after the Norwegian schooner "Axel Thordsen", chartered by A. E. Nordenskiöld's Spitsbergen expedition in 1858.
Albert Bruntoppen	-	a 917-metre peak to the south of Sassenfjorden, named after Jean-Louis Albert Brun, 1851– 1929, Swiss volcanologist, who climbed the peak in 1902.
Amsterdamøya	-	name first used by Dutch whalers in the early seventeenth century.
Arctowskifjellet	-	mountain to the south of Sassenfjorden, named after Henryk Arctowsky, Polish geophysicist who visited Spitsbergen in the tourist steamer "Ile-de-France" in 1910.
Barentsøya	-	island east of Spitsbergen, north of Edgeøya, named after the Dutch navigator William Barentsz.
Bellsund	-	named after the bell-shaped mountain (Klokkefjellet) south of the mouth of the fjord.
Billefjorden	-	innermost, northeastern branch of Isfjorden, named after the Dutch whaler Cornelius Claeszoon Bille, who appears to have visited Spitsbergen in 1675.
Bjonahamna	-	small bay on the north side of Templefjorden, named after the sloop "Bjona" of Tromsø used by the Swedish Spitsbergen expedition in 1882, which mapped and named the harbour.
Bjørnøya	-	the southernmost island of Svalbard. It was discovered by Barentsz's expedition in 1596 who gave it its name (Bear Island) after a polar bear was killed there.

Braganzavågen	-	bay near the eastern end of Van Mijenfjorden, named after Aldegonda, Princess of Braganza (Portugal).
Danskegattet	-	strait between Amsterdamøya and Danskøya.
Danskøya	-	after the Danish whalers who were active in this area in the first half of the seventeenth century.
Dicksonfjorden	-	after Baron Oscar Dickson, of Sweden (1823–1897).
Dickson Land	-	area on Spitsbergen, between Dicksonfjorden and Billefjorden.
Ebeltofthamna	-	harbour on the western shore of Krossfjorden, after Adolph Ebeltoft (1820–1881), lawyer and agent to A. E. Nordenskiöld's Spitsbergen expeditions.
Edgeøya	-	island named after Thomas Edge, British merchant and whaler in the early seventeenth century.
Engelsbukta	-	a fjord on the west of Spitsbergen that was probably an anchorage for English ships or a base for English whalers (English Bay).
Fjortende Julibreen	-	a glacier debouching on the east side of Krossfjorden named after the National Day of France (Fourteenth of July Glacier). The glacier was mapped and named by the expedition organised by Albert I, Prince of Monaco, in 1906.
Flowerdalen	-	valley on the south side of Sassenfjorden, after Sir William Henry Flower (1831–1899), director of the British Museum
Grønfjorden	-	a branch of Isfjorden. The name Green Haven (Green Harbour) was first used by the British in 1610.
Gullybreen	-	glacier to the south of Magdalenefjorden, after its position in a 'gully' between two steep mountains.
Hamburgbukta	-	bay at the northwest corner of Spitsbergen, after the city of Hamburg.
Hinlopenstretet	-	strait separating Spitsbergen from Nordaustlandet
Hopen	-	island to the southeast of Edgeøya, which may have been named after 'Hopewell', the vessel of the English whaling skipper, Thomas Marmaduke, who visited the place in 1613.
Hornsund	-	the southernmost of the large fjords on the western coast of Spitsbergen (23 km long and 8–10 km wide). Named by Poole (1613) who recorded in his diary, "They brought a piece of a Deeres horne aboard, therefore I called this sound Horne Sound".
Hornsundtind	-	mountain, 1431 m, south of Hornsund

Hotellneset	-	a small hotel was built here by the Norwegian shipping company Vesteraalens Dampskibsselskab in 1896.
Hvalpynten	-	the south eastern point of Edgeøya probably named by Edge in 1625.
Ile-de-Francekollen	-	mountain south of Sassenfjorden, after the French tourist vessel "Ile-de-France", which visited in 1906 and 1910.
Isachsenfonna	-	plateau glacier east of Krossfjorden first crossed by Gunnar Isachsen and colleagues in 1906.
Isfjorden	-	called Ice Fjord as early as 1610.
Kapp Thordsen	-	south point of the peninsular between Nordfjorden and Dicksonfjorden, branches of Isfjorden, after the schooner "Axel Thordsen", hired for Nordenskiöld's Spitsbergen expedition in 1864.
Kong Karls Land	-	a group of islands southeast of Nordauslandet named after Karl I (1823–1891), King of Würtemberg (Germany).
Kongsfjorden	-	Norwegian translation of King's Bay and is probably a translation or adaptation of the older Dutch name Koninks Bay (1710).
Krossfjorden	-	northern branch of Kongsfjorden. Name may be derived from a comparison with a cross although has also been explained by the setting up of a cross by the English whaler Jonas Poole in 1610.
Kvalrossbukta	-	bay on the south-east side of Bjørnøya (Walrus-bay).
Kvitøya	-	the easternmost island in the Svalbard archipelago named for its extensive glacial cover (White Island).
Liefdefjorden	-	probably named after the Dutch ship "de Leifde" (Dutch *leifde* = love).
Likholmen	-	small island in Danskegattet, with numerous graves from the whaling period of the 17th and 18th centuries.
Lilliehöökfjorden	-	northwest branch of Krossfjorden, after Commander Gustaf Lilliehöök (1836–1899), member of Otto Torrell's expedition of 1861.
Longyearbyen	-	mining settlement named after John Munro Longyear, 1850–1922, American businessman who pioneered coal mining in Spitsbergen.
Longyeardalen	-	valley southwest of Adventfjorden.
Longyear City	-	see Longyearbyen.

Lusitaniafjellet	-	mountain south of Sassenfjorden, after the English tourist steamship "Lusitania", which visited Spitsbergen with tourists in 1894.
Magdalenefjorden	-	named after the biblical Maria Magdalena.
Marmierfjellet	-	mountain, 709 m, west of mouth of Sassenfjorden, after Xavier Marmier (1809–1892), French author and member of La Recherche which visited Spitsbergen in 1839.
Midterhuken	-	mountainous point, between Van Mijenfjorden and Van Keulenfjorden.
Möllerfjorden	-	eastern, inner branch of Krossfjorden, named after Didrik Magnus Axel Möller (1830–1896), Swedish astronomer and professor at Lund University.
Mosselbukta	-	bay on Spitsbergen east of Wijdefjorden.
Nordaustlandet	-	island to the north of Spitsbergen, the second largest in the Svalbard archipelago.
Nordenskiöldfjellet	-	mountain peak, 1050 m, southwest of Adventfjorden, named after A. E. Nordenskiöld.
Oliviertoppen	-	mountain south of Sassenfjorden, after Dr Louis Olivier (1854–1910), director of Revue Générale des Sciences. Visited Spitsbergen in 1906 and 1910 as one of the leaders of an excursion on board the steamer "Ile-de-France".
Oscar II Land	-	district between Isfjorden and Kongsfjorden after Oscar II (1829–1907), King of Norway and Sweden.
Platåberget	-	mountain between Adventfjorden and Bjørndalen, named after its plateau shape.
Prins Karls Forland	-	after Prince Charles, later King Charles I of Great Britain and Ireland (1600–1649).
Raudfjorden	-	fjord on the northern coast of Spitsbergen, named after the red-coloured rocks along its eastern side.
Recherchefjorden	-	after the corvette "La Recherche" used by a French expedition in 1838.
Recherchebreen	-	large glacier at the head of Recherchefjorden.
Regnardneset	-	headland between Kollerfjorden and Möllerfjorden in Krossfjorden, after Dr Paul Regnard (1850–1927), French physician and physiologist.
Renardbreen	-	glacier west of Recherchefjorden, after "renard" = fox (french).

Roulletegga	-	mountain ridge west of Sassendalen after Lucien Roullet, secretary of the Revue Générale des Sciences.
Sassendalen	-	valley on the southern side of Sassenfjorden.
Sassenfjorden	-	from the Dutch sas = sluice, or basin. Possibly the "basin' where ships can anchor".
Signehamna	-	small bay on the western side of Lilliehöökfjorden, named after Gunnar Isachsen's wife, Signe Amalie Isachsen.
Sjuøyane	-	group of seven islands lying north of Nordauslandet of which the largest are Phippsøya, Martensøya and Parryøya.
Skarvrypehøgda	-	mountain ridge south of the mouth of Sassendalen from the Norwegain word for mountain ptarmigan.
Smeerenburg	-	old Dutch whalers' camp, on the south-east cape of Amsterdamøya. Smeer (Dutch) = speck or blubber, accordingly the name means Blubber Town.
Spitsbergen	-	the largest of Svalbard's islands, named after the Dutch "peaked mountain".
Sorgfjorden	-	fjord west of the northern entrance to Hinlopenstretet
Sørkapp	-	extreme southern point of Spitsbergen.
Skansbukta	-	small bay on the west side of Billefjorden.
Storfjorden	-	large, open fjord between Spitsbergen in the west and Edgeøya and Barentsøya in the east. It is 200 kilometres long and 150 kilometres wide at its mouth.
Svalbard	-	group name of all the islands in the Arctic Ocean which were placed under Norwegian sovereignty by the Treaty of Paris, February 9, 1920.
Templet	-	mountain, 783 m, to the north of Templefjorden after its likeness to a gigantic gothic cathedral fallen into ruins.
Templefjorden	-	innermost branch of Sassenfjorden.
Tinayrebukta	-	small bay in the eastern shore of Krossfjorden, named after Jean Paul Louis Tinayre, 1861– , French painter who visited Spitsbergen with Prince Albert I from 1904.
Torrellbreen	-	large glacier debauching on the west coast of Spitsbergen, north of Hornsund.
Van Mijenfjorden	-	after Wilhelm van Muyden who led the Dutch whaling fleet in 1612–1613.

Virgohamna	-	after "Virgo", the vessel which carried S. A. Andrée to Danskøya in 1896.
Von Postbreen	-	large glacier debauching into the head of Templefjorden. Named after Professor Hampus Adolf von Post (1822–1911), Swedish chemist, geologist and botanist.
Waggonwaybreen	-	glacier debauching at the head of Magdalenefjorden named after the numerous rents in its surface which were likened to the ruts left by a waggon.
Wijdefjorden	-	fjord on the northern side of Spitsbergen, named after the Dutch "the wide fjord".

Bibliography

Primary Accounts

Backlund, Oskar and Arctowski, Henryk. *Dans le Monde Polaire: au Spitzberg et à la Banquise*. Paris, 1910. (*Ile-de-France, 1910*).

Bazin, René François Nicolas Marie. *Nord-Sud. Amérique-Angleterre-Corse-Spitzberg*. Paris, Calmann-Lévy, Éditeurs. 3, Rue Auber, 3, 1913. (*Ile-de-France, 1906*).

Berges, Wilh. *Nordlandfahrt der Auguste Victoria*. Original-photographien. Hamburg, [n.d.] 1898 (*Auguste Victoria, 1898*).

Brosi, Urs. *Eine Fahrt nach Norwegen und Spitzbergen auf dem Doppelschraubendampfer "Blücher" der Hamburg-Amerika-Linie, 1904. Mit 45 abbildungen nach photographischen Aufnahmen und einer Routenkarte*. Zürick, Schulthess & Co., 1906. (*Blücher, 1904*).

Bruch, Margarete. *Mitternachtsonne. Dichtungen von Margarete Bruch*. Berlin, Verlag von Max Schildberger Inh. Arthur Schlessinger, 1912. (*Grosser Kurfürst, 1912* – in verse).

Conway, Martin. *The First Crossing of Spitsbergen*. London, J. M. Dent & Co., 1897.

Cremer, Leo. *Ein Ausflug nach Spitzbergen*. Berlin, Ferd. Dümmlers Verlagsbuchhandlung, 1892. (*Amely, 1891*).

D'Erceville, Henri (Comte). *Un Drame au Spitzberg: l'échouement d "Ile-de-France"*. Journal de bord 23–30 Juillet 1906. Fontainebleau, Maurice Bourges, 1908. (*Ile-de France, 1906*).

Dinckelberg, Hugo. *Nordlandfahrt. Eine reise auf dem Hamburger Doppel-schraubenschnell-dampfler "Auguste Victoria" nach Norwegen bis zum Nordcap und nach der insel Spitzbergen und zwei kaisertage in Bergen*. Hamburg, 1898. (*Auguste Victoria, 1898*).

Dreesen, Wilhelm. *Erinnerungen an meine Nordlandreise 1901*. Flensburg [n.d. ?1902]. (*Auguste Victoria 1900*).

Dubois, Auguste. *Le Région du Mont Lusitania au Spitzberg*. Neuchatel, Imprimerie Attinger Frères, 1911. (*Ile-de-France, 1910*).

Du Boulay, John. *Travels through Spitzbergen, Siberia, Russia &c., and around the seven churches in Asia Minor*. London, The Army and navy Co-operative Society, Ltd. [n.d.]. (*Voyage in 1836*).

Dufferin, Lord. *Letters from High Latitudes; being some account of a voyage in the schooner yacht "Foam", 85 O. M. Iceland, Jan Mayen, & Spitzbergen, in 1856*. London, John Murray, 1857. (*Foam, 1856*).

Frankenstein, A. *Nordlandfahrt bis Spitzbergen mit der "Auguste Viktoria" der Hamburg-Amerika-Linie 1903*. Leipzig, Verlag von Frankenstein & Wagner, 1904. (*Auguste Victoria, 1903*).

Fromholz, Hugo. *Aus Ost und Nord. Reiseschilderungen*. I. Durch Russland. II. Nach Spitzbergen. Berlin, Driesner, 1898 (*Kong Harald, 1897*).

Funke, Alfred. *Eindrücke von der Polarfahrt des dampfers "Grosser Kurfürst"*. Norddeutscher Lloyd. N.d. ?1913. (*Grosser Kurfürst, 1912*).

Gafvelin, Ernst. *Från Spetsbergen och Nordland*. Umeå, Aktiebolaget Umeå Tryckerier, 1911; Svalbardminner nr. 26 Vågemot Miniforlag, 2002. (*Andenæs, 1911*).

Gallois, Eugène. *Une Croisière Française au Spitzberg*. N.p., n.d. ?1907. (*Ile-de-France, 1906*)

Gerard, Adelaide M. *Et Nos in Arctis*. London, Ballantye & Company, 1913. (*Vega, 1913*).

Gerstenberger, L. *Über Island nach Spitzbergen. Polarfahrt auf dem "D Grosser Kurfürst" des Nordd. Lloyd in Jahre 1913*. Frankfurt, 1913. (*Grosser Kurfürst, 1913*).

Hadfield, Philip Hayward. *With the S.S. Ophir (Orient Pacific Lines) on a cruise to Spitsbergen and the fjords of Norway*. London, 1904. (*Ophir, 1904*).

Haffter, Elias. *Briefe aus dem Hohen Norden. Eine fahrt nach Spitzbergen mit dem HAPAG-Dampfer "Auguste Viktoria" im juli 1899*. Frauenfeld, 1899. (*Auguste Victoria, 1899*).

Herz, Ludwig F. *Tropisches und Arktisches. Reise-Erinnerungen*. Berlin, A. Asher, 1896. (*Erling Jarl, 1896*).

Hoenshel, Elmer. *The Cruise of the Neptune*. Staunton, The McClure Company Inc. (*Neptun, 1910*).

Jottrand, Lucien. *Croquis du Nord – Nordland, Finmark, Spitzberg*. Bruxelles, H. Lamertin, Editeurs-Libraire, 1898. (*Lofoten, 1897*).

Kahlbaum, Georg Wilhelm August. *Eine Spitzbergenfahrt*. Leipzig, Barth, 1896 (*Erling Jarl, 1896*).

Kallmorgen, Friedrich. *In's Land der Mitternachtssonne. Tagebuch eines Malers.* Karlsruhe [n.d. 1899]. (*Auguste Victoria, 1898*).

Keilhau, Baltazar Mathias. *Reise i Öst- og Vest-Finmarken samt til Beeren-Eiland og Spitsbergen, i aarene 1827 og 1828.* Christiania, trykt hos Johan Krohn, 1831.

Klinghammer, Waldemar. *Eine Reise nach Norwegen und Spitzbergen auf der "Auguste Viktoria.* Rudolstadt, 1903. (*Auguste Victoria, 1902*).

Lategahn, W. *Eine Nordlandfahrt im August 1893: Reiseerinnerungen aus dem Polarmeer.* Mühlheim/Ruhr: H. Baedeker, 1894. (*Admiral, 1893*).

Leclercq, Jules. *Une Croisière au Spitzberg sur un yacht polaire.* Paris, Plon-Nourrit et Cie, 1904 (*Oihonna, 1904*).

Letellier, Maurice. *A Travers la Norvege et Spitsbergen.* Paris, Lamulle et Poisson, 1897 (*Erling Jarl, 1896*).

Lowenigh, von Barto. *Reise nach Spitzbergen, von Barto von Löwenigh Bürgermeister von Burtscheid.* Aachen und Leipzig, bei Jacob Anton Maher, 1830.

Norddeutscher Lloyd. *Polarfahrt. Zur Erinnerung an die Polarfahrt 1911 mit Dampler "Grosser Kurfürst" 18. Juli bis 16. August.* Bremen, Norddeutscher Lloyd, (*Grosser Kurfürst 1911*).

Norvège-Spitzberg, 10 Juillet au 7 Août 1910. XLIVe Croisière de la Revue Générale des Sciences. [n.d. 1911]. (*Ile-de-France, 1910*).

Phillipps-Wolley, Clive. *The Trottings of a Tenderfoot: a visit to the Columbian fjords and Spitzbergen.* London, Richard Bentley and Son, 1884. (*Pallas, 1881*).

Plass, Friedrich. *Vergnügungsfahrt nach Spitzbergen – Reiseerinnerungen aus den nördlichen Eismeer im August 1893 an Bord des Dampfers "Admiral".* Hamburg, Boysen, 1894 (*Admiral, 1893*).

Schibsted, A. & Resvoll-Dieset, H. *Sommerliv på Spitsbergen 1908.* Svalbardminner nr. 12. Vågemot Miniforlag, 1998. (*Kong Harald, 1908*).

(Seitz). *Erinnerung an die Bade'sche Spitzbergen-Reise, August 1902. Nach aufnahmen von Dr. Seitz.* (*Oihonna, 1902*).

Studley, J. T. *The Journal of a Sporting Nomad.* London, John Lane the Bodley Head, 1912 (*Lofoten, 1896*).

Wegener, Georg. *Zum Ewigen Eise. Eine sommerfahrt ins nördliche Polarmeer und begegnung mit Andrée und Nansen.* Berlin, 1897. (*Erling Jarl, 1896*).

Wilde, Eduard. *Reiseskizzen von einem Ausflug nach Norwegen und Spitzbergen mit dem Dampfer Danzig des NDL im sommer 1895.* Saaz, 1896. (*Danzig, 1895*).

Willburger, Georg. *Mitternachts-Sonne. Eine moderne Polar-Fahrt*. Mit 60 Vollbildern. München [n.d. 1913] (*Grosser Kurfürst*, 1912).

Wiskott, Max. *Nach Spitzbergen bis zum ewigen eise*. Als manuskript gedruckt. Breslau, C. T. Wiskott, 1897.

Wyllie, M. A. *Norway and its fjords*. London, Methuen & Co., 1907 (*Vectis, 1906*).

Zeppelin, Max Graf von. *Reisebilder aus Spitzbergen, Bären-Eiland und Norwegen nach täglichen aufzeichnungen*. Stuttgart, Druck von A. Bonz' Erben, 1892. (*Amely, 1892*).

General Accounts

Adams, Pat, Totten, Alan and Williams, Peter. *Spitzbergen: Cruise Mail 1890–1914*. Scandinavia Philatelic Society, 2007.

Årbok Svalbard 1981-82. Tromsø, 1981

Bay, Arne J. *Svalbard Filatelien*. Oslo, Arne J. Bay, 1979. *Postal History of Svalbard from 1896*. [n.p., n.d. ?2003].

Brown, Rudmose R. N. *Spitsbergen. An account of exploration, hunting, the mineral riches & future potentialities of an arctic archipelago*. London, Seeley, Service & Co., 1920.

Capelotti, Peter J. *By Airship to the North Pole. An archaeology of human exploration*. Rutgers University Press, 1999.

Carpine-Lancre, Jacqueline and Barr, William. *The Arctic cruises of Prince Albert I of Monaco*. Polar Record 2008, 44, 1 14.

Baedeker, Karl. *Norway, Sweden and Denmark. Handbook for Travellers*. Eighth edition. London, 1903.

Dole, Nathan Haskel. *America in Spitsbergen. The Romance of an Arctic coal mine*. Boston, Marshall Jones Company, 1922.

Goldberg, Fred. *Norwegian Postal Service. 100 years on Svalbard*. Sweden, Våstergötlands Tryckeri AB, 1997.

Hamburg-Amerika-Linie. *Nordland = Fahrten. Hamburg-Amerika Linie*. Buch- und Kunstdruckerei A. Wohlfeld, Magdeburg, [n.d.?1905].

Hoel, Adolf. *Svalbard: Svalbard's Historie, 1596-1965*. Oslo, Sverre Kildahl, 1966-67.

Holm, Anders and Thue, Klaus. *Overvintring på Spitsbergen 1895–1896*. Svalbardminner nr. 4. Vågemot forlag, 1997.

Krause, Reinhard A. Im Nordmeer, an den Küsten Grönlands und Spitzbergens: Die Unternehmen des Kapitäns Wilhelm Bade aus Wismar zur Erschließung der arktischen Regionen. In: Guntau, Martin (ed). *Mecklenburger im Ausland. Historische Skizzen zum Leben und Wirken von Mecklenburgern in ihrer Heimat und in der Ferne*. Bremen, Edition Temmen, 2001

Lachambre, Henri and Machuron, Alexis. *Andrée and his balloon*. Westminster, Archibold Constable & Co., 1898.

Lerner, Theodor. *Polarfahrer, Im banne der arktis*. Zurich, Oesch Verlag, 2005.

Matt, Hans von. *Hans Beat Wieland. Leben und Werk 1867–1945*. ABC Verlag, Zürich, 1977.

(Northern Exploration Company). *Marble Island. A short account of the discovery, location and products of the property with practical notes and reports upon the unique variety and values of marbles*. London, Northern Exploration Company, Ltd., 1913.

Norsk Polarinstitutt. *The Place Names of Svalbard*. Tromsø, 2003.

Rüppel, Uwe. *Kapitän Wilhelm Bades Touristikfahrten nach Norwegen, Spitzbergen und ins europäische Nordmeer in polarphilatelister Hinsicht*. Bielefeld, Polarpost-Sammlerverein Bielefeld e.V., 2001.

Scheen, Erland. *Et blad av Spitsbergens Turisthistorie "The Spitsbergen Swindle"*. Oslo, Printed for private circulation only, 1961.

Schøyen, B. and Aune, F. *Katalog over Norges Byposter*, 2005.

Spitsbergen Gazette. Svalbardminner nr. 15. Vågemot Miniforlag, 1999.

Wellman, Walter. *The Aerial Age: a thousand miles by airship over the ocean*. New York. A. R. Keller & Company, 1911.